Khushwant Singh's

More laughs! More laugh

Another super collection
naughty jokes, humorous
interludes, hilarious situations and bitchy remarks,
selected by Khushwant Singh from amongst the
thousands contributed by his readers and fans –
and some manufactured by him. All dedicated to
getting the humorless Indians to smile and to
laugh.

His earlier collection of jokes, *Khushwant Singh's
Joke Book* and *Khushwant Singh's Joke Book II* have
both been runaway bestsellers having sold over
80,000 copies, a rare phenomenon in Indian
publishing. They were widely hailed for "poking
fun at Indians and lampooning politicians". One
reviewer paid a rich compliment by describing the
books as "designed with malice towards one and
all and to give the reader a pain in the belly."

Share a joke with
Khushwant Singh
and a million others.
See page 118
for details.

Khushwant Singh, author and journalist, was born in Punjab in 1915. He was educated at Government College, Lahore, St. Stephen's College, Delhi, Kings College and the Inner Temple in London. He practiced briefly at the Lahore High Court before joining the Ministry of External Affairs. He shot to literary fame with his award winning novel *Train to Pakistan* and the two-volumes *History of the Sikhs*. Subsequently, he edited *The Illustrated Weekly of India* (1969-1979), *New Delhi* (1979-1980) and *The Hindustan Times* (1980-1983) with great distinction. He was a Member of the Parliament from 1980 to 1986. Today as India's best known journalist and widely read syndicated columnist, he enjoys the unenviable reputation of "holding a mirror to our face...of being frank, but not venomous, fearless but not intimidating." According to *India Today*, "Khushwant Singh remains perhaps the most spontaneous commentator and racounteur and has provided Indian journalism with some of its most relaxed, tounge-in-cheek writing."

KHUSHWANT SINGH'S
JOKE
BOOK III

Illustrated by Ranga

Orient Paperbacks
DELHI | MUMBAI | HYDERABAD

www.orientpaperbacks.com

ISBN 81-222-0138-5

1st Published 1992
27th Printing 2004

Khushwant Singh's Joke Book 3

©Mala Dayal

Illustrated by Ranga
Cover design by Vision Studio

Published by
Orient Paperbacks
(A division of Vision Books Pvt. Ltd.)
Madarsa Road, Kashmere Gate, Delhi-110 006

Printed in India at
Rashtra Rachna Printers, Delhi-110 092

Cover Printed at
Ravindra Printing Press, Delhi-110 006

Introduction

*T*he biggest joke is that in a country known to have no sense of humour, joke books have become bestsellers. When the first volume of these series was published neither my publishers nor I had the foggiest notion what kind of reception it would have. It went into nearly two dozen editions within two years. It continues to be reprinted and sold out. The same happened to the second collection. And now we have the third with a totally new collection of jokes sent in by readers or made up by the author. What does that prove? We are not an entirely humourless nation. We may not be able to laugh at ourselves but it does not take much for us to guffaw with laughter at other peoples, foibles and eccentricities. The legacies of Birbal, Tenali Raman and Gopal Bhor have not been lost.

The largest proportion of our jokes continue to be ethnic and based on stereotypes. Marwaris, Banias, Sardarjis, Pathans, Weavers, Haryanavi Jats, Bawajis (Parsis), Mianbhais (Gujarati Muslims), Gujjus (Gujarati Hindus), Makapaons (Goans), Namboodris, Nairs, Bhadralog (Middle-class Bengalis) and many other communities from the staple diet of the humorist. Paradoxically, though most jokes of this genre are made up by members of the communities themselves, they are very touchy about them when narrated by others. Consequently the bulk of ethnic jokes remain an oral tradition and are rarely seen in print. Anyone who publishes them runs the risk of having a lawsuit slapped on him– if not being slapped in public.

The second most popular genre of jokes are against our rulers. India has a long tradition of mocking Kings, Queens, Ministers, Generals and the life in positions of power. Medieval courts had their court-jesters and clowns privileged to speak their minds and were tolerated by these rulers because they were the only means of their finding out what was being said about them by the people. As a matter of historical fact, a large portion of our traditional folk humour is about foolish Kings, Ministers and Commanders being cuckolded by their wives. The more tyrannical the rule, the more underground humour it generated. The tradition has gone down history and every dictator from Adolf Hitler, Mussolini and Stalin down to Zia-ul-Haq of Pakistan were the butt of jokes. Mrs. Indira Gandhi came in for a fair share when she imposed Emergency on the country and locked up thousands of her political adversaries. A good example is the very first entry in this compilation.

Besides these, there are the usual anecdotes about servants, thick-headed peasants, funny slogans written behind scooters and trucks (a uniquely northern Indian phenomenon), quarrelsome wives and naive Sardarjis. In some ways this volume has a richer variety of *desi* humour than its two predecessors. I hope you will get plenty of laughs out of it.

Khushwant Singh

Emergency

*T*his happened during the Emergency imposed by Mrs. Indira Gandhi in 1975. Bapu Gandhi, up in heaven, was troubled by the thought that after all he had done for his country, no one even remembered his name. He sent for Jawahar Lal Nehru and said "Nehru *beta*, you ruled the country for many years. What did you do to perpetuate the memory of your Bapu Gandhi?"

"Bapu, I did everything I could. I had a *samadhi* built on the spot where we cremated your body. On your birthdays and death anniversaries we gathered at the *samadhi*, sang *Ram Dhun* and *Vaishnav Jan*. What more could I do?"

"Who came after you?" asked Bapu.

"I am told Lal Bahadur became Prime Minister after me," replied Nehru.

So Bapu Gandhi sent for Lal Bahadur and put him the same question. Shastri replied: "Bapu, I had a very short time as Prime Minister – only one and a half year, but I had your statues put up in every town and village. I had all your speeches published in all languages and distributed free. What more could I have done?"

"Who came after you?" asked Bapu.

"It's Nehru's *chhokree*, Indira. She is now ruling India."

So Bapu sent for Indira Gandhi, who had just imposed Emergency on the country and put the same question to her. Indira Gandhi replied: "I have done more to perpetuate your memory than either Shastri or my father. I have made the entire country like you. I have left the people nothing more than their *langotis* and a staff like you have."

Bapu was horrified. "*Beti*, this is very wrong. The people will rise against you for depriving them of

9

everything."

"Not to worry, Bapu," replied Indira. "I have taken care of that. I have put the *langoti* in their hands and put the *danda* up their bottoms."

Santji and His Chela

*T*his happened after the assassination of Mrs. Gandhi. It might be recalled that her assassin Beant Singh was killed a few minutes after he had committed the foul deed.

Beant Singh arrived in the presence of Bhindranwale and reverently touched his feet. "*Santji*, I have done the job you assigned to me. I have killed the woman who ordered desecration of the Golden Temple and gave you martyrdom."

"You have done well," said Bhindranwale. "Ask for any reward and I will give you."

"*Santji*, I have nothing to do. Please find me good job," pleaded Beant Singh.

"Ask for any job and I will arrange it for you," replied Bhindranwale.

"*Santji*, all I know is guarding V.I.Ps. Please appoint me as your security guard."

Bhindranwale had second thoughts. "*Puttar*, ask for some other job. I cannot appoint you as my security guard."

A Nation of Clerks

*T*wo tigers disappeared from the Delhi zoo. Not a trace could be found of them anywhere. Then suddenly one day six months later, they were back in their cages. One was skin and bones; the other had put on a lot of weight. They began to compare notes. Said the thin tiger: "I was very unlucky. I found my way to Rajasthan. There was a famine and I couldn't find anything to eat. The cattle had died and even the humans I ate had hardly any flesh on them. So I decided to get back to the zoo. Here at least I get one square meal every day. But you look healthy enough. Why did you come back?"

Replied the fat tiger, "To start with I was very lucky. I found my way to the government secretariat. I hid myself under a staircase. Every evening as the clerks came out of their offices, I caught and ate one of them. For six months no one noticed anything. Then yesterday I made the mistake of eating the fellow who serves them their morning tea. Then hell broke loose. They looked for him everywhere and found me hiding under the staircase. They chased me out. So I am back to the zoo. It is safer here."

Short Call

*M*rs. Banta Singh was in the habit of having long conversations on the telephone, sometimes going on over an hour. One day she hung up after 25 minutes. "What is the matter today?" asked her husband. "Today you had less than half an hour conversation on the phone."

"I got a wrong number," replied Mrs. Banta Singh.

Contributed by J.P. Singh Kaka, New Delhi

Murdered English

*H*ere are examples of some charming misprints.

In Pune Cantonment they have a separate mess for officers of the Intelligence Bureau. The signboard reads "Intelligence Mess".

Again in Pune, a devout truck driver has printed behind his vehicle: "God is grate." Another warning overtakes "Horn Blow". And a butcher advertises his wares as "Farash meet of Pork sold here".

The best is the signboard on a bakery:
"Bakery Number One
Dilruba & Sons
The biggest loafers in town."

Contributed by U.C. Hakeem, Bareilly

Look Like Yourself

*S*een outside a barber's saloon near a bus stop is the following message:
"Visit immediately, no time waste
Instant Beauty Saloon
Special visiting hours from 5.30 p.m. to 7.30 p.m.

If you are a passenger alighting from buses in the evening hours then walk straight into our saloon. We make you up-to-date so that your wife and children recognise you without difficulty!

Preferable: A copy of your original photograph for matching!"

Contributed by G. Gopalakrishnan, New Delhi

Small Time Thief

A boy was caught stealing a watch from a shop. He was taken to a police station and put in a lock-up. A hardened criminal lodged there showed some sympathy and said, "You are wasting time on small items. Why don't you rob a bank?"

The boy replied, "By the time I leave school, all banks are closed."

Contributed by P.S. Chawla, Chandigarh

13

Bachelors Not Allowed

*I*n the good old days, when people had to walk long distances from one place to another, travel came to a halt at sunset. The traveller had to ask for shelter for the night. The request was generally granted.

One such young traveller finding himself in a strange town late in the evening knocked at a door and asked for one night's stay. The old man snapped back, "Sorry, young man, we have young *bahus* and *betis* in this house. Try next door." He tried next door. This house also had young *bahus* and *betis* and the young man was asked to try the next door. He tried a number of houses and to his dismay, he got the same answer everywhere.

Dejected and tired, he desperately tried yet another door. Even before the owner could open his mouth, the young man asked, "Excuse me Sir, do you have young *bahus* and *betis* in your house?"

"Yes, why do you ask?" enquired the master suspiciously.

"I want to spend the night here," replied the young man.

Contributed by Shekhar Dey, New Delhi

Suspense Story

*R*amesh asked his classmate "Do you know how to keep a *bewakoof* (dunce) in suspense."

"No, you tell me."

"I'll tell you another day."

Contributed by Sandeep Kulshreshta, Agra

Prayer, Counter-prayer

*B*anta Singh had a bitter quarrel with his wife. In his anger he prayed loudly *"Hey Bhagwan! mujhey uttha ley* – Lord take me away from this world."

Mrs. Banta Singh retaliated: *"Hey Bhagwan! mujhey uttha ley."*

Banta Singh quickly amended his prayer: *"Hey Bhagwan! tu iskee sun lay* – O Lord, grant her prayer."

Contributed by J.P. Singh Kaka, New Delhi

Thou Shalt Not...

A padre lost his bicycle. He was very distraught and consulted a friend about what to do. "It must be a member of your congregation who took it," said his friend. "Next Sunday after your sermon, read out the ten commandments. When you come to 'thou shalt not steal'; pause and take a good look at the congregation. The one who stole it will look guilty and you will be able to spot him."

The following Sunday the friend asked the padre if he had found his bicycle. "Yes, indeed," replied the padre, "its back with me."

"So you followed my advice and found the guilty man?"

"In a way," replied the padre. "When I came to 'thou shalt not commit adultery', I suddenly recalled where I had left it."

Contributed by Zakia Kidwai, New Delhi

Telephone Call

*O*nce a doctor got a telephone call in the middle of night. The caller sounded very excited. "Doctor, please come at once. My wife is in great pain and I am sure it is appendicitis," he said. The doctor assured him that there was no need to panic. "I will come in the morning." The man protested, "But doctor, my wife is really serious." The doctor replied, "I took out your wife's appendix two years ago. She can't have another." The caller protested, "That is alright doctor, but now I have got another wife!"

Contributed by R.N. Lakhotia, New Delhi

Auto Lingo

A Sardarji newly arrived in England, brought a car before he picked up the language or rules of the road. One day while driving in the countryside his car skidded off the road and landed in a ditch. Much as he tried, he could not get it to move forward or backward. An Englishman passing-by who came to help him asked, "What's the matter, mate?"

The Sardarji replied in his best English, "My car *garhey mein phasing*. Not *hilling aggey*, not *hilling picchey*, only horn *pee-pe karing*."

Contributed by Shivtar Singh Dalla, Ludhiana

16

Golden Wedding

*O*n my walk every morning I meet a group of septuagenarians narrating jokes and experiences of their younger days.

One morning I heard one of them announce that it was his golden wedding anniversary that day. The consensus was that, the occasion demanded a celebration. The suggestion was mooted that the group should contribute towards the celebration and allow the honoured couple the pleasure of re-enacting their wedding.

One of them volunteered to set up a *pandaal* and illuminations. Another offered to serve dinner; the third agreed to put up the *vedi* for *pheras* and bring a priest. The fourth, after some thought said, "All this is fine, but who will do what is supposed to be done after the *pheras*?"

Contributed by Sohindar S. Rana, New Delhi

Fouled Proposal

*B*anta fell in love with a college girl but did not know how to propose marriage to her. After much thinking he asked, "Sujata, would you like to be the mother of my children?"

Sujata replied, "Why not? How many have you?"

Contributed by Sandeep Kulshreshta, Agra

Sun Downer

Santa: "*Yaar*, where does the Sun go at night?"

Banta: "It does not go anywhere. It remains there but due to darkness we can't see it."

Contributed by J.P. Singh Kaka, New Delhi

Double-Bounty

When God created the world, he could not help boasting to *Brahma* of the special favours he had bestowed on India. "I gave it the highest mountains and the broadest rivers in the world; I gave it enormous forests teaming with wild life; I gave it coal, gold and diamond mines. I gave it the best of everything."

"Was it fair to give one country so much wealth?" asked *Brahma*.

"You should see the kind of people I put in India. They will waste everything I gave them."

Contributed by K.L. Dutta, Dehra Dun

Winner Takes All

Banta Singh was telling a friend, "Yesterday my wife and I had a terrible quarrel. I wanted to go to the club; she wanted to go to the movie."

"Which film did you see?" asked his friend.

Contributed by J. P.Singh Kaka, New Delhi

18

Mixed up Knowledge

*H*ere is an amusing account of an oral general knowledge test in school. The teacher asked, "What was the name of the last Vicereine of India and what was her hobby?"

A girl replied, "Mountess Countbatten. Her hobbies were mounting and counting studs."

Contributed by Francis Dean, Ranchi

Matrimonial Preference

*T*here was a time when I used to carefully scan matrimonial advertisements, not to look for a wife but just to find out what others were looking for in their life-partners. I gave up wasting my time on them many years ago. When I casually glance at them I am surprised to find they are dividing the categories by caste, profession and nationality. The latest categorisation has been brought to my attention by T. R. Rishi; apparently living in South Delhi has acquired status of acceptability. Three ads from *The Hindustan Times* state clearly "residing in South Delhi. Preference for South Delhiites." One adds a clarification "affluent South Delhi family".

Committee meetings: One person gets up and speaks and says nothing; nobody listens. Then everyone disagrees with the speaker.

Parents: People who have pictures in their wallets where money used to be.

A factory owner says: Old accountants never die – they just loose their balance.

Contributed by Dr. Gauri Shanker Mukherjee, Kanpur

"*T*he Bible says that the cow chews the cud. But this is false according to Biology," said a boy to a Christian priest. The priest retorted, "Theology is not Biology! Praise the Lord!"

Contributed by K.J. Mathew, Kerala

A minister went to the school where his son was a student to enquire about his son. When the principal told him that his son was poor in all subjects, was very shy and did not mix with children, the minister replied, "I am not worried about his being poor in learning. What I am worried about is that he is shy." The principal looked puzzled. The minister continued after a pause, "Do whatever you can to make him bold and free from shyness. He is to become a minister. For that he must be bold and free from shyness. Once he becomes a minister, he will be a master of all subjects."

Contributed by K. J. Mathew, Kerala

One chimpanzee studying the palm of another: "I see a grim future for you. You're going to evolve into a man."

Contributed by Amarpreet Nagra, Patiala

A Hindu *Bauji* was a neighbour of a Sardarji. Every morning *Bauji* was in the habit of playing guitar along with his son outside his house, which was a disturbance to Sardarji. One morning, *Bauji* was playing it as usual, then Sardarji came out and asked. *"Kee gal Bauji, suvere suvere bajaun lag jande ho?"* *Bauji* replied back in taunting mood, *"sikhni ju hoee"*. Sardarji felt it, and asked *Bauji* (pointing at *Bauji's* son) *"eh vee sikh da ha?"*

Contributed by Ranjit Singh, Kausalya Ganj

*O*n a rain-soaked night, an infant tumbled over the railings of the Howrah bridge and fell into the Hooghly river below. The weather did not prevent hundreds of Calcuttans from flocking over the rails and watching the proceedings, but no one attempted to save the drowning child. At last an old American tourist jumped into the water and did the saving. Later, when he was being interviewed by the radio and T.V.; complimented on his bravery and asked to say something; he roared at them saying, "Bring forward the rascal who pushed me from behind."

Contributed by Kaushik & Kanishka Datta, Calcutta

*A*t the New Year's eve party at a fashionable hotel a girl was overheard talking to her boy friend, "Don't get tense and be worried Micky – when I told you that I was going to be a mother, I only meant yours. Yes, next month I am going to marry your father."

Contributed by R. N. Lakhotia, New Delhi

A young, enthusiastic Family Planning official was deputed to gauge the success of the Family Planning message in rural Bihar. He reached a remote village which proudly housed a family of eight children.

On reaching the house, he saw the father lazily enjoying a *hookah* in the shade of a neem tree. In a dignified manner the official introduced himself, and asked "Sir, hadn't you thought about our Family Planning methods before you had these eight kids!"

"Why should I?" he replied angrily. "The methods are all useless!" jeered the hefty Bihari.

"But, Sir, have you tried using condoms?" enquired the official.

Without responding to his question, the Bihari called two of his children rolling in the dirt. "*Oye*, Bablu, Dablu, come here!" Then he addressed the official. "Can you see them! They are the result of a torn condom!"

Saving his pride, the official replied, "Ok, Sir, you could have tried Copper-T."

"*Oye* Lallu, Kallu, come here!" he called.

"Can you see them! They came out of their mother's womb with the Copper-T in their hands!" he quipped.

"OK, Sir, leave alone Copper-T and condoms. You could have tried pills! After all, they are very convenient and effective!"

"*Oye*, Bolu Cholu, come here!" and two more came running. "Can you see them? They were born after my wife took those godamned pills!"

"OK, Sir, forget everything," quoted the official, trying to repair the faltering image of his department, "at least you could have practised self-restraint!"

"*Oye* Bali, Vali, come here," called the Bihari.

"Can you see them!" he asked smilingly and continued, "they are the result of self-restraint."

Contributed by G. R. Srinivas Murthy

Once a couple had one of their usual quarrels; as a consequence of which, all conversation between them stopped. Unfortunately the husband was to attend his office very early the next morning. So he wrote on a piece of paper, "Please wake me up at 6 a.m. tomorrow morning," and kept it beside his wife's pillow.

His wife read it and went to sleep.

He woke up very late the next morning and got very angry. He looked ferociously at his wife, but she calmly pointed towards his pillow. Under his pillow he found a piece of paper. On it was written, "Please wake up, it is 6 o'clock now."

Contributed by Rizwan Yasser, Calcutta

Two Sardarjis lived in a multistoreyed building, one on the first floor and the second on the eighth floor. But there was great enmity between the two. Once the Sardarji on the eighth floor tried to fool the Sardarji living on the first floor by calling him for dinner. When the Sardarji reached the eighth floor for dinner he saw that the house of his neighbour was locked and a board was hanging on the door, on which was written: "*Kaisa ulloo banaya*" (How have I fooled you!) The Sardarji felt embarrassed and turning the board to the other side, wrote: "*Main to yahan aayaa hee nahin tha*" (I had never come here)."

Contributed by Anand P. Kothawala, Ahmedabad

A signboard on a *halwai* shop reads: "Credit only to those above 85 if accompanied by both parents."

Contributed by Anupama Joseph

*T*wo bachelors were talking about their respective choice of life partner. One friend said, "It is generally said that people with opposite characteristics make the happiest marriages. What is your opinion?" The friend replied, "Yes, they are right. That is why I am looking for a girl with money!"

Contributed by R.N. Lakhotia, New Delhi

*O*n the first day, in a kindergarten, the young Miss introduced herself and was teaching the kids how to remember her name. "Now, listen, my name is Prussy – it is pussy with an R in it."

Next day, she asked one of the kids whether he remembered her name. The boy replied "Yes, madam, your name is Crunt!"

Contributed by S.B. Iyer, Bangalore

A young woman had given birth in the elevator of a New Delhi hospital, and was embarrassed about it. One of the nurses, in an effort to console her, said, "Don't feel bad. Why, only two years ago a lady delivered in the front yard of the hospital."

With that the new mother burst out crying. "I know," she said, "that was me, too."

Contributed by Vijay Kayal, Hojai

*Y*oung lady: "My husband is always telling me to go to hell. I would like to know if I could legally take my children with me."

25

*T*he school Inspector asked the class whether he should ask one difficult question, or two simple questions. A clever student told him to ask only one difficult question. The Inspector asked him the place where the first woman was born. The boy answered that it was at the Lady Hardinge Hospital, New Delhi. "How do you know?" the Inspector asked. "No second question, please," the boy triumphantly replied.

Contributed by Baldev Kapur, Delhi

A Sardar walked into a household appliances store. The owner was busy tallying his accounts and his eyes were glued to his ledgers. The Sardar asked the owner "I want that VCR." Without taking the eyes off the ledgers, the owner replied, "No, Sardar, that is not for you."

Our Sardar felt insulted. He thought that the shopkeeper was biased against Sardars. Next day, he arrived at the shop clean shaven and without his headgear. He asked for the same VCR. The owner, who was again busy tallying his accounts replied without raising his head, "No, Sardar, that is not for you."

The Sardar was perplexed. How could the shopkeeper guess correctly that he was a Sardar? So, the next day, the Sardar went to the same shop disguised as a woman, in *churidar* and *pyjama*, head covered with *dupatta*, and asked for the same VCR. The shopkeeper again replied without raising his head — "No, Sardar, that is not for you!"

Puzzled, the Sardar asked the shopkeeper how he guessed that he was a Sardar without raising his head. "Very simple," said the shopkeeper. "That is not a VCR. That is a washing machine!"

Contributed by S.B. Iyer, Bangalore

Paradisal Justice

*T*hree men who died the same day were presented before God. The almighty showed particular interest in their sex life. The first one replied that he never had an affair before or after he was married. God granted him a chauffeur-driven Cadillac. The second man admitted he had some affairs before he was married but none afterwards. God gave him an Ambassador car. The third man confessed to having had lots of affairs. God gave him a scooter. A few days later the man with the scooter saw the fellow with the chauffeur-driven Cadillac sitting by the roadside and crying. The scooterist asked him why was he upset. Replied the Cadillac owner, "I've just seen my wife ride past on a bicycle."

Contributed by D.K. Saxena, Jaipur

A mother and her convent-raised young daughter were riding in a taxi one evening through a midtown block notorious for early hour street solicitation. "What are all these women waiting for, mother?" the girl asked.

"They're probably meeting their husbands there after work," replied the woman hastily.

"Aw, c'mon lady," grumbled the taxi-driver, "why don'tcha tell her the truth? She's young enough."

"Please mom," said the girl, "I want to know."

Looking daggers at the back of the driver's head, the woman carefully explained the situation. When she had finished, the daughter asked, "But, what happens to the babies those women have?"

"They grow up," the woman replied, "and become taxi-drivers."

Contributed by Vijay Kayal, Hojai

*J*awaharlal Nehru once visited the Sarhand Club, Ambala Cantt., sometime in 1958. At the dinner party the food had been laid on the table for self-service. An officer, taking little notice of the Chief Guest's presence, put a good chunk of chicken on his plate and started eating hastily. Standing behind him, Nehru was watching this officer and then to everybody's amusement, gave a soft pat on his shoulder and said, "*Aahista khao, murda hai, bhag to nehin jayega*" (Eat slowly, it is now dead and can't escape).

Contributed by Baldev Kapur, Delhi

*E*mperor Akbar was bending down to pick up a couple of coins that had dropped from his pockets when Birbal tiptoed behind him and administered a harmless tap on the royal behind. The king leaped up, and when he came down was in such a rage that he ordered Birbal's execution. When he calmed down slightly, however, he announced that Birbal would be given his freedom if he could come up with an excuse more outrageous than the original act.

Birbal promptly said, "As a matter of fact, I didn't know it was you – I thought it was the Queen."

Contributed by Vijay Kayal, Hojai

*B*ald Man: A person who has lot of face to wash and very little hair to comb.

Contributed by Vijayalakshmi Sai Ram, Nagpur

*A*n important politician was seen moving around with a film actress for a couple of months, with whom he finally decided to plunge into matrimony. But, being cautious, he hired a private detective for the job of looking into her antecedents and finding out if she had any previous affairs with men.

After a few days, the politician, at last, received his detective's report which went like this: "Sir, this lady has a spotless reputation. Her past is clear; her family and friends all come from a very respectable background. No one has anything against her character. But yes, according to the grapevine, for the last couple of months she's been frequently seen flirting with a politician with a dubious reputation."

Contributed by Shashank Shekhar, Meerut Cantt

A colleague recently visited Kulu Manali. He was so overwhelmed by the scenic beauty that he wired his wife — WISH YOU WERE HERE.

On his return the poor chap had to face a hostile atmosphere and a furious wife. Reason? A distorted message reading: WISH YOU WERE HER!

Contributed by O.P. Bajaj, Jabalpur

Q: "If a Negro servant were to let fall the principal dish of the Christmas plate, how will the world be affected?"

A: "The fall of Turkey, the breaking-up of China, the over-throw of Greece and the humiliation of Africa."

Contributed by A. V. Menon, Bangalore

A Japanese tourist arrived in New Delhi. While travelling in a taxi, he happened to observe that everything in India moved at a slower pace compared to his own country. Unable to contain himself, he said to the taxi-driver, "Your taxis are too slow, Japanese taxis go very fast. Look at your buses, they ply at a snail's pace. In Japan, buses run like hell. Look at the speed of your motorcycles. Japanese motorcycles seem to talk to the air."

At the end of the journey, the taxi fare amounted to Rs.100.

"What!" exclaimed the furious Japanese "your taxi-metre runs too fast."

"Yes, why not?" spewed the taxi-driver. "It's after all made in Japan, Sir!"

Contributed by Shashank Shekhar, Meerut Cantt

*T*his relates to an I.A.S. officer who could read, write and even speak English. He once gave a 'very good' report of his subordinate officer, writing in his Confidential Report that the officer 'hardly works'. It was only after the officers' representation that the reporting officer clarified that he meant the officer was hardworking. When the same officer once went to inspect a B.S.F. picket on Gurdaspur border, he made these brief remarks on the Visitors' Book: "Jawans are healthy, horses are happy, I am glad." Interestingly, when a foreign dignitary was being shown round his residence, our English-speaking officer took the dignitary to the back of his house, saying, "These are my private parts."

Contributed by Baldev Kapur, Delhi

*I*t was evening and Natha Singh sat in the drawing room of the house of his uncle in Jalandhar. Natha Singh was almost all dressed up. He had his socks and shoes on. The turban was nicely tied and the beard was neatly rolled up. He had a necktie around his neck. But he was in his vest and underpants only. Entered his uncle and asked, "Natha, you are sitting almost dressed up, what goes?"

Replied Natha, "Uncle I am dressed up, because someone may drop in."

"But you are in your vest and underpants only," exclaimed the uncle.

"Sometimes no one drops in," replied Natha Singh.

Contributed by Raj Bir Singh, Calcutta

*D*r. T. M. Nair, a well-known politician of Madras of the early nineties, while in London used to frequent a particular pub in the East End. His usual drink was a cocktail of vermouth and gin, the code word for which between his regular waiter and himself was virgin. Once in the absence of the regular waiter, the one substituting for him came to take Dr. Nair's orders. "The usual virgin", Dr. Nair said. After a minute or two, the waiter came back and whispered into the ear of his client, "One cannot be found in London at present, Sir."

Contributed by A. V. Menon, Bangalore

*Q*ueen Victoria wrote to a grandson who had a reputation for wild, reckless squandering, urging the virtue of thrift. "Dear Grandma," he wrote back, "thank you for your kind letter of advice. I have sold it for $10."

Contributed by Amit Banerjee

*T*wo nuns of Christian Mission in the city were cruising leisurely along one misty morning in their Mission's newly acquired Maruti Gypsy when they ran out of fuel. The driver of a passing lorry agreed to give enough petrol, to enable them to proceed to the nearest petrol station. The only container the nuns had with them was a bedpan, and they collected the petrol in it. While filling the tank, a car came by and stopped. Its driver, a good-looking, well-dressed young man got out and came over. Cheerfully, he said, "Young ladies, any trouble? Any help needed?" The nuns replied, "Thank you, Sir, we ran out of fuel, we are just filling our tank." The young man stood looking for a second, stunned. He threw his hands up and said, "Oh, glory be to the Lord...faith, nothing but faith."

Contributed by A. V. Menon, Bangalore

*F*rom one Sardar to another:

S-1: "How many *rotis* can you eat on an empty stomach?"

S-2 : "Why four!"

S-1: "Oh, what a fool, once you have taken one *roti*, you are no more with as empty a stomach as when you started."

S-2 has a hearty laugh at himself.

Not to be outdone, S-2 goes home to confront his missus with the same query as S-1. The missus is very busy mixing *atta* for the night meal and in disgust, upon the insistence of her Sardar, answers angrily, three *rotis*.

S-2 is upset. If only the missus had said four there could have been a good joke!

Contributed by N. Anantaraman, Calcutta

A customer came to the Special Assistant of a Bank (who had a poor knowledge of Hindi) in connection with the payment of a fixed deposit of his deceased father. He said in Hindi.

Customer: "*Mere pitaji gujjar gayen hein. Mein yeh* fixed-deposit *ka* payment *lena chahata hun* (My father has died. I want the fixed deposit receipt to be encashed)."

Special Assistant: "*Unka* signature *to chahiye* (His signature is required)."

Customer: "*Woh to gujjar gayen hein* (He is already dead)."

Special Assistant: "*Gujjar gayen hein to kya hua? Kabhi to wapas ayenge* (He has gone to Gujjar. Some day or other he will be back)."

Customer: "*Woh to mar gayen hein. Kaise ayenge?* (He is already dead. How will he come?)"

Special Assistant: "*Mar gayen hein to pahale se kyon nahin batayen?* (Why didn't you say at first that he had died?)"

Contributed by Subhashis Ray

*I*n a family the greatgrandfather, grandfather, father, and the son who was a little child were all found to be liars. However, since the greatgrandfather was a politician, it was in his nature to tell lies; since the grandfather was a lawyer, he was professionally required to tell lies; and since the father was a doctor, he had to lie to his patients. Only the poor child seemed to have no excuse.

Contributed by Gaurav Johar, Amritsar

34

A man, heavily drunk, went to church on a Sunday, few minutes before the Mass began. The priest who was standing outside the church, asked him, "Don't you know that it is a sin to come to church after drinking alcohol?" The man replied coolly, "I know that, Father. I have come to confess, to purge my sins."

Contributed by K.J. Mathew, Kerala

A drunk, after having had one too many, called up the bartender and asked him the distance between Dalhousie Square and Ballygunge in Calcutta. The bartender, in all honesty, answered, "Why, Sir, it is 15 kilometers." The drunk then asked him the distance between Ballygunge and Dalhousie Square, which again the bartender answered as 15 kilometers. Whereupon the drunk accused the bartender of being heavy on the booze, asking how his answers could be correct a Monday to Friday and Friday to Monday could not be the same distance.

Contributed by N. Anantaraman, Calcutt

*T*he late ASP Iyer, ICS, was president of the prestigious Music Academy of Madras. For the Annua Day of the Academy, Mr. Keskar, the then Minister fo Information & Broadcasting was invited to preside. The Hon'ble Minister came in one full hour behind schedule and began with profuse apologies for being late. He began, "You must be all waiting for me..." Said ASP Iyer "Please do not worry, Sir, we were waiting for ou coffee."

Contributed by A. V. Menon, Bangalor

*T*he warden was making his usual round at the asylum and saw one of the inmates holding a fishing rod He had the end of the rod dangling in the washbasin Trying to be kind, the warden asked, "Catch anything?"
The inmate replied, "In a washbasin? Are you crazy.'

Contributed by Kamal Sharma, Mukeria

*A*t an intermediary station on the Bombay route, wo mail trains for Bombay and Delhi pulled up. The tation being a meal-halt, the trains stopped for a long while; a Sardar, heading to Bombay, got into the wrong rain. going to Delhi. In it he confronted another Sardar.

After the initial *Sat Sri Akaals*, one asks the other the estination and each gives the same. The person on the wrong route, then exclaims "Oh, what progress India has nade! Same train, same compartment, same cubicle, one erth goes to Delhi and the other to Bombay!"

Contributed by N. Anantaraman, Calcutta

*O*nce a Jat went to Bombay. While passing through road he saw a very high building. He was amazed to ee it, and decided to count its stories. As he was doing o a townsman saw him and tried to befool him. So he pproached the Jat and asked, "What are you doing?" When he was told the answer the townsman said that ne had to pay two rupees for every storey counted. How many have you counted?" The Jat said ten and ave the man twenty rupees. Walking away the Jat was ery happy to think how he has befooled the other man, or he had counted twenty.

Contributed by Anupam & Pranav Anshumali, Patna

*T*here was a Sardarji who was running a business Delhi with branch offices at Ambala and Amritsar. O day he decided to visit his branch offices, and boarded night train. He kept himself awake till 2 a.m., and whe the train reached Ambala at 2.20 a.m., he was fast aslee and woke up only when the train reached Amristar. H was unhappy, but decided to visit Ambala on his wa back to Delhi. Again he boarded a night train, and kej himself awake till 3 a.m., but when the train reache Ambala at 3.30 a.m., he was fast asleep, and woke u only when the train was steaming into Delhi. Th happened three to four times. He was either landing u at Delhi or at Amritsar, always missing Ambala k sleeping off. So naturally he got worried.

He narrated his problem to a close friend who sai "You are a rich man, so why don't you travel by 1st clas The coach attendant will wake you up, a little befor Ambala, and you can travel in comfort." The advice wa logical, and was accepted.

So he arranged his reservations in 1st class and o the day of journey, boarded the train and sought out th conductor. As luck would have it, the coach attendar too was a Sardarji. The businessman Sardarji explaine his predicament to the conductor, imploring him to, necessary, throw him out of the train at Ambala. O being reassured by the attendant that his wishes woul be honoured to the letter, went to sleep.

And lo and behold, when he got up, he foun himself at Amritsar, and was expectedly furious. H caught hold of the attendant, and started raining blow abuses and choicest endearments in Punjabi. Thi resulted in a big crowd gathering around them. Peopl were astonished to see a railway employee being treate thus on railway platform, with the railway employee no summoning the railway and police authorities.

After exhausting himself fully, our friend took his baggage and left the station. The crowd, not able to curb their curiosity asked the conductor the reason for his submitting to such an insult in public without a whimper. The attendant in his most hurt way said, "I can understand this Sardarji getting agitated by my not helping him to detrain at Ambala, but I still, for the life of me, cannot see the reason, why the other Sardarji, whom I had physically thrown out of the train at Ambala, was also furious and abusive."

Contributed by Ranbir Mehta, Nasik

A foreigner came to stay at his Indian friend's home and expressed a wish to see rural India. On their trip through the farmlands, fields and riversides, the foreigner complained about the habit of people sitting everywhere on their haunches and manuring the land. The patriotic Indian vowed revenge and when he went abroad to stay with his friend, he also wanted to see the rural landscape. The picturesque land with spotlessly clean fields and farmlands put out the Indian until suddenly he leapt up in the air seeing a man in the distance in a familiar posture. He was gleeful until he and his friend drove near only to find the Indian ambassador to the country.

Contributed by Kaushik & Kanishk Datta, Calcutta

*D*octor: "Did that medicine I gave your uncle straighten him out?"
Man: "Yes, they buried him, last week."

Contributed by Kamal Sharma, Mukerian

39

*O*nce Prem Singh went to England. In the evening he went to attend a party given by Margaret Thatcher in a marvellous house. As he was passing through a gallery of that house, a guard stopped him and fined him with fifty pounds for smoking, as smoking was prohibited there. Prem Singh searched through his pocket but he had only a hundred pound note. So he asked his secretary, "Sharma, you smoke too."

Contributed by Anupam & Pranav Anshumali, Patna

A barber's neighbour frequently went to his shop, wished him, and inquired about the time it would take for his turn to come and walk away. After this ritual went on for some time the barber grew suspicious and followed his neighbour. The gentleman was found in barber's house with his better half literally following the commandment "love thy neighbour".

Contributed by Kanti C. Singhee, Chittorgarh

A merchant asked a sailor, "Where did your father died?"
"He drowned at sea."
"And your grandfather?"
"At sea too."
"Aren't you afraid of the sea?"
The sailor retorted, "Where did your father died?"
"In bed."
"And your grandfather?"
"In bed too."
"Aren't you afraid to go to bed every night where your father and grandfather died?"

Contributed by V. C. Jacob, Ranchi

A drunkard was coming home from a local liqour shop late at night. He lived alone and locked his house whenever he went out.

As he neared his house he took out his key to open the lock, but he could not manage to put the key into the hole.

After trying this repeatedly, he was tired.

A neighbour who was witnessing the scene took pity on him and said, "Give me the key I will get it open for you."

The drunkard looked for a while, and said to him, "The lock will be opened by me, but do me a favour, please hold the house firmly, while I do the rest. Damn it, it is shaking like a pendulum."

Contributed by Vaishali Nithyananda Rai, Mangalore

*O*n leaving his office and reaching the tram stop, a Sardar found that the tram bound for his home had just started moving. The Sardar, in his anxiety to get home fast, ran after the tram; in course of time, it was found that the race between the speeding and slowing tram and the Sardar ended with the Sardar reaching home, chasing the tram.

Gleefully, the Sardar exclaimed to his wife upon entering home that he has saved up 40-paise that day chasing the home-bound tram! The Sardarnee, however, was not amused, but quite upset, and said, "After all you are only a Sardar – instead of chasing the tram, if only you had chased a taxi, you could have saved ten rupees instead of a mere 40-paise."

Contributed by N. Anantaraman, Calcutta

41

*I*n his autobiography, *Treasure in Clay*, Bishop Fulton Sheen tells of getting lost in Philadelphia on his way to a lecture at the Town Hall, "I stopped to ask a few boys for directions. They told me where the Town Hall was and then asked, 'What are you going to do there?'

'I'm giving a lecture on heaven and how to get there. Would you like to come and find out?'

'You're kidding,' one boy said. 'You don't even know the way to the Town Hall.'"

Contributed by Surjan Singh, Dhanbad

*T*he new *bahu* demurely told her mother-in-law, "*Ma!* I want to know about the customs here." The mother-in-law, pleased, said, "Yes. Yes. Go ahead!" "How many months after marriage are babies delivered here?" the *bahu* enquired. "Why, after nine months," told the mother-in-law, struck by her *bahu's* innocence. "But," declared the *bahu*, "in my father's place, they do it after six months, and for the first time I shall follow their custom."

Contributed by Kanti C. Singhee, Chittorgarh

*O*ne morning Santa Singh received a letter in the post warning him, "If you do not send Rs. 50,000 to the above address immediately, we will kidnap your wife and you will never see her again."

Santa Singh sent the following reply,

Dear Sir,

I do not have Rs. 50,000 but your offer interests me greatly.

Contributed by Kamal Sharma, Mukerian

Banta Singh was in court charged with parking his car in a restricted area. The judge asked him if he had anything to say in his defence.

"They should not put up such misleading notices," said Banta Singh. "It said, FINE FOR PARKING HERE."

Contributed by Rajan Sharma, Mukerian

A girl who was appearing in B.Ed. got married. The result of B.Ed. was declared when she was in her in-laws house. She had secured the first position and in her excitement she sent a telegram to her father.

SUCCESSFUL IN B.ED

Due to the efficiency of the telegraph department, the father got the telegram as: SUCCESSFUL IN BED

The father cursed the daughter for sending this telegram about her conjugal affairs.

Contributed by Sushil K. Bhatia, Panchkula

A doctor got a call from a very excited woman, "My son just swallowed ten aspirins, what'll I do?"

He replied, "Give him a headache, what else?"

Contributed by Vijay Kayal, Hojai

Banta: "*Yaar* Santa, last night I had a wonderful dream, I saw I was getting married."

Santa: "Last night I also had a wonderful dream. I saw I was getting divorced."

Contributed by Rajib Bhattacharjee

43

A man, showing off his knowledge to another, asked if he knew what shape the world was.

"I don't know," said the second. "Give me a clue."

"It is the same shape as the buttons on my jacket," said the first.

"Square," said the second.

"That is my Sunday jacket," said the first. "I meant my weekday jacket. Now what shape is the world?"

"Square on Sunday, round on weekdays," said the second man.

Contributed by Rajan Sharma, Mukerian

*A*n American and a Russian archaeologist were bragging to a Sardarji. The Russian said that while digging an ancient ruin in Russia he came across some thick cables; therefore he claimed that the Russians had the telegraph system long before it was invented. The American said that while digging a ruin in America he found thin cables. This indicated that his ancestors used telephones. Now the Sardarji spoke. He said that while digging ruins in India, men could find nothing; no cables, no wires. It clearly proved that his ancestors used the most sophisticated wireless system.

Contributed by T. T. Subhashini, Ahmedabad

*S*anta Singh was walking on the road and paused to read the graffiti on the wall.

It read *"Padne waala gadha."* (One who reads it is an ass.)

Santa Singh thought for an hour, erased it and wrote back, *"Likhene waala gadha"* (One who wrote it is an ass).

Contributed by Sunil Gogia, Hyderabad

44

A Managing Director was interviewing a charming lady for the post of Personal Secretary. Finally he asked the lady what salary she expected? Very modestly she replied "Rs. 2500, Sir." "With pleasure," said the Managing Director. "In that case Rs. 3500, Sir," was the prompt reply by the lady.

Contributed by Surjan Singh, Dhanbad

A notorious tiger was on the prowl, terrorizing a village. So the villagers held a high level meeting to put down this tiger menace. A brave Sardarji stood up twisting his moustache and flexing his muscles, "I can tackle this maneater single-handed," he boasted. "Give me a cowhide and remember," he roared, "not a single soul should venture out tonight. Leave the rest to me." Now, disguised as a cow he stood as a bait waiting to ambush the tiger. Hours passed; suddenly the villagers heard someone screaming in great agony. They all dashed to the spot, only to find the Sardarji lying on the ground groaning and bleeding profusely. One of them asked the Sardarji, "What's the matter? Did you manage to kill the Tiger?" Already the villagers had begun shouting, "Sardarji *jindabad*, Sardarji *jindabad*."

"Stop, you idiots, traitors," he screamed. "Tell me first whose bull was it, whose bull was loose tonight!"

Contributed by T. T. Subhashini, Ahmedabad

"*A* dog is a very faithful animal."
"Yes, I also believed the same before I met you."

Contributed by Surjit Sethi, Dimapur

*L*ehna Singh was taking a stroll on a moonlit night when he saw a man searching for something on the ground.

"Hey, what are you looking for?"
"My ring, Sir," he replied.
"Did you lose it here?"
"No, Sir, over there, under that tree. But it is brighter here so I am looking for it here."

Contributed by Rajib Bhattacharjee

*O*nce, a couple living in our neighbourhood was found quarrelling among themselves quite often. One day my neighbour Mr. Sharma asked Mr. Gupta why they quarrelled so much. Mr. Gupta replied that he and his wife enjoyed quarrelling and getting angry. Mr. Sharma was astonished and asked Mr. Gupta to explain. He said that during quarrelling his wife throws the rolling pin at him and if it hits, then she is happy and if it happens to miss then he is happy and taunts her over her failure.

Contributed by Sushil K. Bhatia, Panchkula

A Buddhist and a Hindu were once good friends on the earth. When they died, they both went to heaven. Since the Buddhist arrived first, he began to show the Hindu around. The Hindu was very impressed. He asked many questions. Soon they came to a large hall. The Buddhist ordered the Hindu to be very quiet as they tiptoed past it. "Why did you ask me to be quiet when we passed that hall just now?" soon enquired the Hindu.

"Well, it's because I did not want us to be seen," explained the Buddhist. "That hall belongs to the Christians. They think they are the only ones in heaven. So I felt it better not to disillusion them."

*A*n American and a Russian were arguing about the virtues of communism and democracy.

"C'mon man!" said the American, "In a democracy you get to express your views. You have freedom. You know, I can anyday call President Bush an idiot!"

"What's so great about that," said the Russian, unimpressed "so can I!"

*I*t was the Irish chess championship and the two Irish grandmasters were sitting with their ·heads bent over the board, contemplating their strategies. Radio, television and the newspapers waited with bated breath for the next move. Hours went by and there was no sign of anything happening. Then one of the grandmasters looked up and said "Oh, is it my move?"

Contibuted by Rajan Sharma, Mukerian

*F*our persons were waiting for the Shatabdi Express at Bhopal railway station, the train was half-an-hour late. They started talking to each other.

First man: "I am a colonel, I am married. I have three sons and all of them are doctors."

Second man: "I am also a colonel. I am also married. I have also three sons and all of them are engineers."

Third man: "I am also a colonel. I am also married, I have also three sons and all of them are lawyers."

The fourth man was quiet till he was asked about his family.

Fourth man: "I am not a colonel. I am unmarried, but I have three sons and all of them are colonels."

Contributed by Vivek Khara, Bhopal

*M*r. Sen and Mr. Singh were two good friends. Mr. Sen was thin and Mr. Singh was fat.

Mr. Singh: "*Yaar* Sen, seeing you, outsiders would think that there is a famine in India."

Mr. Sen: "And seeing you, they would come to know the cause of the famine."

Contributed by Rajib Bhattacharjee

*O*nce there was a competition to decide who was the best milkman. The only rule to be followed was that the person would be locked inside a chamber and could take his own sweet time with the cow, milking her.

First was the turn of an American who went in and came out with thirty litres of milk after two hours.

Then a Russian went in, and came out with forty litres in four hours.

Then a Japanese even got better of the two, and an Australian who after a full ten hours got eighty litres of milk.

Now it was the turn of Banta Singh, who proudly went in with his animal and did not come out after one whole day, and people could hear him abuse the animal in his own language. Then after a lapse of 1½ days Banta came out with a small glass of milk and people started laughing at him.

An embarrassed Banta remarked *"Oye, twanu sab no a gau milee si, manu ta baal phada ditaa"* (You all got a cow to milk what I got was an ox and see what I have done.)

Contributed by Madhuker Pathey, Delhi

*T*his happened to an American visitor in Madras. In his hotel room he picked up the telephone one night and asked for a 7-Up. The switchboard operator answered in his best English, "7-Up? Yes, Sir."

The cold drink never arrived, but the next morning the tourist was woken up punctually at seven o'clock.

*A*t a world conference, the heads of states of all countries were boasting about their technical know-how. So they all decided that to prove their boasts, each country should show an engineering feat to the world. In a few days, the U.S.A made a hollow tube of fibreglass, a millimeter in diameter. It was then sent to the Russia. They put a conducting wire in the tube. The Japanese, to prove their superiority, bored a hole through the wire. Finally, it was sent to India.

It came back without any apparent change.

"Well, what have you done?" asked everybody.

"Look here," said the Indian, putting the wire under a microscope. Clearly visible were the words "Made in India".

Contributed by J. S. Pannu, Thane

*A*Sardarji was travelling in a train without ticket. The T.C. of the train was also a Sardarji. When the travelling Sardarji saw the T.C. Sardarji coming he thought of an excuse which he had heard from other people, that is, ministers can travel free. So when the T.C. came and asked this Sardarji for his ticket, he said "*Oy! asi minister.*" The T.C. asked aback "*Oy! tusi kade Minister*"(which minister). The poor Sardarji couldn't think of any minister except Mrs. Indira Gandhi, so he said "*Oy! asi Indira Gandhi.*" Immediately the T.C. caught the traveller Sardarji's feet for blessing and said "*Oy! asi bauth sunya, oh! asi bauth padya, aaj dhek leya.*" (I heard a lot about you, I read a lot about you and my luck, I saw you today.)

Contributed by Dr. Pramon Parmar, Jaipur

*A*t an international seminar where scientists were boasting about their countries' achievements, an American scientist claimed that they had invented a fighter plane which could touch the ceiling of the sky. When challenged, he admitted that it didn't actually touch it, but almost did. Then a Russian scientist claimed that they had invented a submarine which could travel on the floor of the sea. He was also challenged and he had to admit that the submarine almost travelled on the floor. The Indian scientist then claimed that they were now able to feed themselves through their nose. He was also challenged. He then said, "Well, almost."

Contributed by Pankaj Shukla, Unnao

*O*nce Santa Singh and Banta Singh happened to be together in Delhi. Having excursion tickets, they boarded a DTC double decker. Banta Singh, finding no vacant seat in the lower deck, went to the upper deck and took a seat. He was surprised to see that there was no driver in the upper deck. Showing his anxiety, he asked Santa Singh if there was a driver in the lower deck. Promptly came the reply that there was indeed a driver. Banta Singh then said *"Utte te wahe guru challanda pia hai"* (God is driving this upper deck himself).

Contributed by M. L. Aneja, Karnal

*I*n cricket if you hit and run you will be rewarded. In a car accident if you hit and run you will be punished.

Contributed by Vijayalakshmi Sai Ram, Nagpur

51

A successful husband is one who earns more money than his wife can spend.

A successful wife is one who can find such a husband.

Contributed by Sunil Gogia, Hyderabad

"*W*ake up– wake up, darling."
"What happened?"
"Nothing. I just forgot to give you sleeping pills."

A man was passing a house where a sign was posted: BEWARE OF THE CANARY. He saw the house owner outside, watering the lawn, and asked, "Why should anyone beware of a canary?"

The house owner simply replied, "This one whistles for the dog."

Contributed by Lawrence Miller

*W*inston Churchill and Abraham Lincoln are both famous for their wit and superb sense of humour.

Once they happened to meet on a staircase which was not wide enough for both of them to pass. Churchill stood in the middle of it and said to Lincoln, "I don't give way to a fool." Lincoln promptly stepped aside, allowing Churchill to move and replied, "Well, but I do, your excellency."

Contributed by Birendra Mohan Pandey, Bhagalpur

A Sardarji went to the doctor to get some medicine as he was not feeling well. "This is pretty strong stuff," said the doctor, "So take some first day, then skip a day, take some again and then skip another day and so on."

A few months after the doctor met Sardarji's wife and asked how he was.

"Oh, he is dead," she told him.

"Did not the medicine I prescribed do him any good?" asked the doctor.

"Oh the medicine was all right," she replied. "It was all that skipping that killed him."

Contributed by Rajan Sharma, Mukerian

*C*ustomer: "Waiter! I asked for *Alu Paratha* but I find no potatoes in it!"

Waiter: "What's in a name Sir! If you ask for *Kashmiri Pulav*, will you expect to find Kashmir in it?"

Contributed by Rajib Bhattacharjee

*T*he husband was always busy pouring over books. The nagging wife once said with a sigh, "If I were a book, I could always find your company." The husband promptly replied, "Dear, if you were really a book, you should be an almanac, so that I can change it every year."

Contributed by Ardhendu Sanyal, Calcutta

*S*tepping out from her bathing tub, a lovely young woman was reaching for a towel when she became aware of a window cleaner looking at her. So stunned was she that she couldn't move a muscle. She just kept staring at the man.

"What's the matter, lady?" he said, "Haven't you seen a window cleaner before?"

Contributed by Amarpreet Nagra, Patiala

*T*he other day, after inaugurating the newly-built Medical College in New Delhi, the Hon'ble Health Minister was delivering the speech:

"...since the attainment of Independence, India has made a tremendous advancement in the arena of medical sciences. Thanks to the assiduous efforts of Indian scientists and doctors, we can now boast of new inventions, sophisticated surgical instruments and modern medical facilities, which no other country in the entire world can. It is a matter of immense pride that we have truly outclassed America, Britain, France, Germany, Spain and other advanced nations. An enviable achievement indeed, of which we all should be proud! Well, dear brothers and sisters, I don't wish to prolong my talk. In fact, I cannot, as you know that I've been plagued by a spinal-cord problem for the last week or so. And, I have to be leaving for New York shortly for my medical treatment."

Contributed by Shashank Shekhar, Meerut Cantt

54

Once two friends were boasting about themselves.

Banta Singh: "Once my grandfather's wrist-watch fell into a well. When it was pulled out after thirty years it was still running."

Santa Singh: "So what is so great about it? Once my grandfather himself fell into a well, and after thirty years when he was taken out, he was still alive."

Banta Singh: "How can it be possible? What was he doing in the well for thirty years?"

Santa Singh: "Why not? He was winding your grandfather's wrist-watch."

Contributed by Rizwan Yasser, Calcutta

A lazy angler cast his line but was hardly taking any notice of the float going down. A passerby seeing this could not resist pulling the string, and caught a good fish. "Thank you," said the angler, "would you bait the hook and cast it for me please." The man did so, but said, " I wish you had a little child to take care of such things." The lazy fellow thought for a while and said "I am a bachelor. By the way, any idea about a pregnant bride?"

Contributed by D. L. Das, Bilaspur

A man was seen walking in a drunkard manner, with anger writ large on his face, wearing a pair of somewhat tight shoes. A Haryanavi passerby who happened to go that way, stopped and asked the man, "From where did you buy such tight shoes?"

"Ae Mister, you had better mind your own business I've plucked them from a tree! But I wonder what's that to do with you."

"Absolutely nothing. But friend, you made some haste. If you had plucked them two or three months hence they would have definitely fitted your feet well," said the Haryanavi mockingly.

Contributed by Shashank Shekhar, Meerut Cantt

*B*rowsing in a bookstore, a woman found a book she knew would please a friend. As she was about to hand it to the clerk, she noticed that the jacket was soiled.

"Isn't this a little dirty?" she inquired.

"Ma'am," the clerk replied impatiently, "how should I know? I don't have time to read books."

Contributed by Lawrence Miller

Ditto To You

A Sardarji and his son who ran a modest motor spare-parts business won Rs.50 lakhs in a lottery. They spent the money to expand the business to include spare-parts for imported cars. They placed orders with foreign firms and got invoices in return. They were foxed by the language: "Excel 929, two pieces. Price $90." The line beneath read: "Ditto, eight pieces, price $360."

They could not understand what "ditto" meant. So the father went to consult a friend who explained what the word meant. The father returned to his show-room and conveyed the meaning of the word to his son: "*Main haan ullu da pāttha. Tey toon hain ditto.*" (I am son of an owl and you are ditto).

Contributed by H. Bahal, Agra

Learned Learner

*S*ardar Tehl Singh, an emigrant in Canada, earned enough money to buy himself a brand new car. He drove out of the sales depot with an L-plate on the car. As the car zig-zagged down the main highway, a traffic cop picked him up "Why are you going from one side of the road to the other?" he demanded.

"I am learning how to drive," replied Tehl Singh.

"You have to have a driving teacher beside you. May I see your licence?"

Tehl Singh pulled out an envelope from his pocket and replied, "Here, I am learning driving by correspondence."

Contributed by Shivtar Singh Dalla, Ludhiana

57

You say your mother-in-law threw a chair at you?" said the Magistrate.

"Yes Sir."

"And then your wife threw a table, but what made you leave the house?"

"I saw my wife looking thoughtfully at the side board."

One night, Banta was walking homewards when a thief jumped on him all of a sudden. Banta and the thief had a terrific tussle. They rolled about on the ground, and Banta put up a tremendous fight until, at last, the thief managed to get the better of him and pinned him to the ground.

The thief then went through Banta's pockets and searched him all over. There was only a 25-paise coin he could lay his hands on. The thief was so surprised at this that he asked Banta why he had bothered to fight so hard just for a 25-paise bit.

"Was that all you wanted?" said Banta Singh, "I thought you were after the five-hundred rupees I've got in my shoe!"

Contributed by Shashank Shekhar, Meerut Cantt

From a Babe's Mouth

"Daddy, are you scared of the dark?"

"No son, who told you I was frightened of the dark?"

"No one. But why do you then creep into Mummy's bed at night?"

A mediocre Haryanavi lad somehow managed to reach the finals of a boxing competition. At the final encounter, he had to face a tough Jat from Uttar Pradesh who happened to be a former heavyweight champion. When the Haryanavi boxer was proceeding towards the ring where the much-awaited bout was to take place, it was noticed that he hung back.

"C'mon– It's all right," said the Haryanavi's coach with a view to boosting his morale. "Just say to yourself 'I'm going to knock him out' and see, you'll be the ultimate winner."

"That's no good, Sir," replied the hopeless Haryanavi boxer. "*Manne malum sai ki mein kitna jhoota sai* (I know what a liar I am)."

Contributed by Shashank Shekhar, Meerut Cantt

*I*n an international exhibition a stall exhibited some packets containing brains of men of different races with price tags varying widely from Rs. 1,000 to 1,00,000. A visitor enquired about the content of the packets, and he was told that those were the brains of the men of famous races like Rajput; Jat; Sardar; Bengali; Marwari etc. He then asked why a particular brain cost so high. "You see this is the 'Sardarji's brain' which is so rare that you get not more than one out of hundred skulls," explained the man at the counter.

Contributed by D.L. Das, Bilaspur

Love Thy Neighbour

A young couple moved into a new house. The wife was attractive but aloof. Being unable to hold out any longer, the eager neighbour once spotted her hanging her washing, and said "*Behenji*, your cow has eaten up my marigolds."

"That can't be true," protested the pretty neighbour. "We don't have a cow."

"I don't have marigolds either," replied the smart aleck, "but I don't like so much distance between neighbours."

Contributed by P. S. Chawla, Chandigarh

Only Asses Do It

A man much harassed by his wife took his four-year-old son to a zoo to escape nagging at home. They came to an enclosure where a donkey was grazing. "Papa, what is this animal?" asked the boy.

"This son, is an ass."

The next enclosure had a she donkey. "And what is this?" asked the child.

"This son, is the wife of an ass."

"Papa, do asses also get married?"

"Han beta," replied his Sire, *"Sirf gadhey hee shaddi kartey hain*– only donkeys get married."

Contributed by Alok Gupta, New Delhi

*T*he wife wanted to do some shopping during the day and so, at breakfast, she asked her husband for a hundred rupees.

"Money, money, money!" he shouted at the top of his voice. "Every day of the week you want more money. If you ask me, I think you need brains more than you need money."

"Perhaps so," his wife agreed, "but I asked you for what I thought you had the most of."

Contributed by Shashank Shekhar, Meerut Cantt

A patient suffering from a nasty cold visited Dr. D'costa and said, groaning, "Doctor, can you cure my terrible cold? It has made things hell for me for the last four or five days."

Having never read about any confirmed cure for common cold, the young, over-zealous doctor advised after much initial hesitation, "You may do one thing. Take a hot bath and stand beneath a fan."

"Stand beneath a fan!" perplexed by the strange instruction, the patient asked, "Will your method cure me, doctor?"

"I can't say so for sure," replied Dr. D'costa, with his spectacles resting on his nose, "but if you do as directed, you are certain to get pneumonia which I can cure for sure!"

Contributed by Shashank Shekhar, Meerut Cantt

*T*o escape the scorching heat of the plains, the big guns of the government during British rule used to move up to Shimla for almost five months, from mid May to mid-October. The Viceroy and his large retinue always travelled by a special train which left Delhi at night and reached Kalka early next morning. Tight security was maintained all along the line and every station master was required to send a telegraphic message to Delhi as soon as the train passed his station. Of particular importance was the railway bridge over river Ghaggar near old Chandigarh (now called Chandi Mandir) where the train usually arrived at about 4 a.m. The old station master there used to spend a sleepless night from tension. There is a story that once in typical railway English, he sent the following telegram after the safe crossing of the train over the bridge: "His Excellency passed away peacefully."

Contributed by P. S. Chawla, Chandigarh

*T*he announcement of the Professor's new book on Astrophysics and his wife's new baby appeared simultaneously in the newspaper. Upon being congratulated on the 'proud event in the family', the Professor naturally thought of the achievement that cost him the greater effort.

"Thank you," he replied modestly, "but I couldn't have done it without the help of my two graduate students."

Contributed by Shashank Shekhar, Meerut Cantt

Natha Singh and Prem Singh, two carpenter friends, were doing a job in a gallery to be set up for an exhibition of paintings by Satish Gujral.

Now during the lunch break, these two carpenters had a couple of drinks. When they resumed work, one of them got hold of a nail, climbed the stool and placing the head of the nail on the wall started hammering on the pointed side of the nail. Realising that the nail was not going in, he had a close look. He still held the nail with its head resting on the wall. He pondered for a while and then called out to his companion, "Oh, Natha Singha, come and see. The person who has manufactured this nail is a fool. He has made this nail upside down."

Natha Singh came and saw Prem Singh holding the nail with its head against the wall. He exclaimed, "It is you who are a fool. This nail is meant for the wall on the opposite side." He caught hold of the nail in the position it was in, took it to the other wall and hammered it in.

Contributed by Raj Bir Singh, Calcutta

*N*ow these two carpenter friends in due course made some money. Hearing that there was demand and money for carpenters in England, they started to learn a bit of English.

After some time they decided to migrate to London.

While boarding the Air India plane at the International Airport at Delhi, Natha Singh had both his hands full. In one hand he carried a tin of pure *ghee* and in the other a small bag containing pulses, *papars, waries* etc. As he climbed the gangway, the beautiful air hostess welcomed him with folded hands.

Natha Singh put down the *ghee* tin and the bag and folded his hands to return the greetings and said; "*Sat Sri Akal, kurey, par mein tenno pachayana nai*" (*Sat Sri Akal* girl, but I have not been able to place you.)

Contributed by Raj Bir Singh, Calcutta

*A*fter a number of years in England Natha Singh decided to visit his native village in Punjab. But he decided to spend a few days in Bombay and then a day in Delhi to pay homage in the Bangla Saheb Gurdwara near Connaught Place.

He landed in Bombay and a friend received him. He enjoyed his sightseeing in Bombay and after a couple of days boarded a train for Delhi. He went into deep sleep in the train. This train reached Bhopal at about 8 a.m. Someone in the compartment put on the radio. And the

Hindi newsreader's voice said, *Yeh, Dilli hai*. This woke up Natha Singh. He got up hurriedly, collected his bags, got down and went out of the Railway Station. He got into a cycle rickshaw and told the puller to go to Bangla Saheb Gurdwara near Connaught Place. Now this clever muslim rickshaw puller of Bhopal smiled to himself, and was on his way.

After two hours the rickshaw puller, with a worried look told Natha Singh that he had lost his way and would like to ask someone for direction. Saying this he got of and went to a nearby teastall and started having tea while telling the joke to other rickshaw puller.

In the meanwhile Natha Singh was getting nervous and impatient. Luckily, he saw another Sardarji coming his way in a rickshaw. Natha Singh ran towards him and requested him to alight to listen to him in private, out of the hearing of his rickshaw pullers.

This Sardarji nodded wisely and got down and listened to Natha Singh's woes.

Natha Singh explained in a whisper. "You know, my rickshaw puller seems to be a rogue. He has been taking me for a ride. Two hours ago I started in his rickshaw from the Railway Station for Connaught Place to go to Bangla Saheb Gurdwara and now he says he has lost his way."

"You have become impatient in two hours," said the other Sardarji. "I have been in my rickshaw for the last ten hours to go to Karol Bagh and my rickshaw puller has not reached Karol Bagh."

Contributed by Raj Bir Singh, Calcutta

Tailpiece

*T*here is this particularly good one about the Soviet Union doing the rounds these days. For one whole day, a worker was stealing parts from a pram factory. He started assembling them. No matter how he attached one part to another, the result was the same – a machine gun.

*A*nother one from the USSR:
A nurse at the kindergarten tells children, "In the Soviet Union, the workers have everything they want; everything belongs to them. Their children have plenty of food and toys." Little Vanechka burst into tears, "I want to go to the Soviet Union."

Widow's Might

*C*ensus Officer: "*Mataji*, you say your husband died six years ago but you have given the names of two sons aged four and two years respectively."
Widow Lady: "I said my husband died six years ago. I didn't say I also died at the same time."

Contributed by Rajnish, Giri Naga

*A*n avid angler caught a little fish of some kind. He held the poor thing in his hand, looked at it for a while then threw it into the water, saying, "Now go home, but want you here tomorrow with your parent."

Contributed by D.L. Das, Bilaspu

Respectability

*B*anta Singh was staying in a five star hotel. One evening, seemingly upset, he walked up to the desk clerk and asked, "Is this a respectable hotel?"

"It is, Sir!"

"Well," said Banta, "I was on the fifth floor and I saw a naked man chasing a naked woman down the corridor."

"Did he catch her?" asked the desk clerk.

"No."

"Then, Sir, it's still a respectable hotel. *Wo hath to naheen aayee*– she was not caught."

Contributed by Shashank Shekhar, Meerut Cantt

From Washington

*M*y friend sent me these jokes doing the rounds of the American capital since President Bush and his lady moved into the White House and vice president Quayle has turned out to be somewhat of a nincompoop. It is said that Millie, the President's dog (bitch), is being banished from the White House because she pisses on the Bushes and eats Quayles.

Since in the absence of the President, a vice president automatically steps up, the Democrats are calling for a Quayle-Bush impeachment insurance.

Also that the secret service be given standing orders that if someone shoots President Bush, they should first shoot vice president Quayle.

There are no limits to American black humour.

Contributed by Amir Tuteja, Washington

Bofors Brand

I happened to be in Stockholm on a business trip last month and was dining in a restaurant. Before ordering my dinner I asked for a whisky.

"Which is the best Swedish whisky?" I asked the waiter.

"Sir, are you from India?" he asked.

"Yes."

"Then you must try our very special brand 'Bofors', it gives you instant kickbacks."

Contributed by Sanjay Jain, Dehradun

Tit For Tat

*D*octor: "I'm sorry to say that the cheque you gave me has bounced back."

Banta: "It is right doctor, so has my fever."

Contributed by J. P. Singh Kaka, New Delhi

Touch

*I*t is entirely wrong to say that Mr. Khushwant Singh is a habitual drinker. He drinks only on two days—one when it rains and other when it does not rain.

Contributed by Dr. D. K. Saxena, Jaipur

Heard in Germany

*T*his is the latest joke doing the rounds in Frankfurt, since East and West Germany were united. A Frenchman, a Scotsman, a West German and an East German met in a restaurant to celebrate. The Frenchman ordered a bottle of champagne and poured it out to his friends. The bottle was only half-empty when he tossed it out of the window. "Why did you do that?" asked the others. "Not to worry," replied the Frenchman "we have plenty of champagne in France and can afford to waste some."

The Scotsman ordered a bottle of premium brand Scotch and filled four glasses. Following the Frenchman's example, he tossed the bottle, still half-full, out of the window. "Why did you do that?" asked his companions. "Not to worry," replied the Scotsman, "there is plenty of Scotch available in my country. Wasting some doesn't make much difference."

It was the turn of the West German. He didn't know what to offer his friends. So he picked up the East German and threw him out of the window. "Why did you do that?" asked his astonished friends. "Not to worry," replied the West German, "we have more East Germans than we need. One less won't make much difference."

Contributed by Harjeet Kaur, Germany

A Haryanavi peasant came to the office of *The Hindustan Times* to place an advertisement announcing his father's death. "The rate is Rs. 360 per single col. cm.," the clerk told him.

"Main to lut jaoonga – I'll be ruined," exclaimed the Haryanavi. "My father was 182 cms tall."

Contributed by J. P. Singh Kaka, New Delhi

Ulta-Pulta Definitions

*M*arriage: An institution in which a man loses his bachelor's degree and a woman gets her master's.

Politician: Someone who chose politics because he discovered it to be the most promising of all careers – and he was always good at making promises.

Doctor: A person who cures your ills by pills and kills you by his bills.

Shaving: An exercise that is performed on the face from time to time to get rid of the excess blood that gets accumulated there.

Alimony: A mode of payment that enables a woman who at one time lived happily married to live happily unmarried.

Cheat: A person for whom, when he borrows money, it's not only against his principle to pay interest, but also against his interest to pay the principle.

Contributed by Shashank Shekhar, New Bombay

Ranga

A Sardarji was travelling in a train. The ticket collector came and asked him to show his ticket. The Sardarji politely asked, "Which one should I show, the one in my right pocket or the one in my left pocket?" The T.C. was taken aback. He then said, "Show me the ticket in your right pocket." The Sardarji promptly showed the ticket. It was perfectly in order. The T.C. then requested the Sardarji to show the ticket in his left pocket also. That was also in order. The T.C. then asked for the reason for buying two tickets. The Sardarji explained, "If someone picks one pocket then I have the other ticket left." The T.C. asked again, "Suppose someone picks both your pockets, what happens?" The Sardarji said with a smile, "I have a third ticket inside my *pugree*."

Contributed by Dr. N. N. Laha, Gwalior

Poetic Justice

A man suffering from severe constipation went to consult a doctor. The doctor prescribed a laxative. It did not work. When the man turned up again the next day to complain of the medicine's ineffectiveness, the doctor prescribed a strong purgative. It had no effect either and the man turned up for something more effective. "What do you do for a living?" asked the doctor.

"I am a poet. I write Punjabi poetry," replied the man.

"Your trouble is not constipation," said the doctor, "there is nothing in your stomach to be evacuated. Take these ten rupees and get something to eat."

Contributed by A. S. Deepak, Chandigarh

Message For The Youth

A father and son were discussing the speech to the Nation made by the new Prime Minister, Mr. Narasimha Rao, highlighting, inter-alia, various economic problems facing the country. The father emphasised the importance of the role of the youth and told his son, "My son, our country has great faith in your generation. Just look at the size of the national debt we expect you to pay."

Contributed by R. N. Lakhotia, New Delhi

Time Bomb

*T*wo terrorists were driving their Maruti to the spot where they intended to place their bomb. The one in driver's seat looked very worried. "Natha, what happens if the bomb we have on the back seat blows up before we get to the site?"

"Not to worry," replied Natha, "I have a spare one in my attache case."

The Lantern Bird

*O*n retirement from the army, Kaka Singh and Bhola Singh settled in adjoining villages on the Kalka-Simla highway. One day Kaka Singh invited Bhola Singh to dinner to meet his visiting relations from London. Bhola Singh thought that as the path was steep it would be useful for him to take a lantern with him for use on the return journey. The party went on very well till about midnight, with a lot of wining and dining. Bhola Singh left in a jolly mood and reached home safely in the early hours.

The next morning there was a knock on the door. "Kaka Singh sent me to enquire whether you reached home safe and sound last night," the servant said. With a smile, Bhola Singh replied, "Oh yes. There was no problem."

The servant then said, "Sir, you left your lantern at our place; instead you brought along the cage of our parrot with you. I have come to return your lantern and take back the cage."

Contributed by P. S. Chawla, Chandigarh

73

Family Problem

*T*wo men met at a bar and struck up a conversation. After a while one of them said, "You think you have family problems? Listen to my situation. A few years ago I met a young widow with a grown-up daughter and we got married. Later, my father married my stepdaughter. That made my stepdaughter my stepmother and my father became my stepson. Also my wife became mother-in-law of her father-in-law. Then the daughter of my wife, my stepmother had a son. This boy was my halfbrother because he was my father's son, but he was also the son of my wife's daughter which made him my wife's grandson. That made me the grandfather of my halfbrother. This was nothing until my wife and I had a son. Now the sister of my son, my mother-in-law, is also the grandmother. This makes my father the brother-in-law of my child, whose stepsister is my father's wife. I am my stepmother's brother-in-law, my wife is her own child's aunt, my son is my father's nephew and I am my own grandfather and you think you have family problems!"

Contributed by Atul Kumar, Sahibabad

One Upmanship

A shop near the district court put up a sign-board bearing these words. "Letters typed in three languages."

The next day a rival shop across the road displayed a bigger board saying: "Photostat copies prepared in all languages."

Contributed by Romilla, Chandigarh

Mesalliance

A lady ant proposed marriage to an elephant. "Marriage!" scoffed the tusker, "don't be silly! How can I marry you?"

The lady ant pleaded with him but to no avail. Then she asked him to bend down so that she could whisper her secret in his ear to persuade him to accept her proposal. The elephant knelt down to hear what she had to say. "The reason why I want you to marry me now is that the child I am carrying in my womb is yours."

Contributed by Suneeta Budhiraja, Noida

The Right Address

*N*otice on the board outside a church in Delhi read, "If you are tired of sinning, come inside." Beneath it somebody added, "If you are not, then come and see Neeloo, House 10, G. B. Road."

Contributed by J. P. Singh Kaka, New Delhi

Indo-Pak War

*O*ne taxi driver in Lahore to another, "Did you hear that the Pakistan government bought a thousand septic tanks?"

The other driver replied, "Yes, and as soon as they learn to drive them, they're going to invade India."

Metric Conversion

*A*n officer from the weights and measures department was giving a lecture on the metric system. He ended with the words, "From now on, I want you to think millimetres, talk millimetres and dream millimetres – every inch of the way."

Contributed by Reeten Ganguly, Tezpur

Brave Names

"*W*ho is it?" asked the inmate of a house when he heard a knock on his door.

"I am Sher Singh," came the answer.

"Sher Singh who?"

"I am Sher Singh, son of Dilawar Singh."

"Who is your grandfather?"

"Bahadur Singh."

"Why don't you come in? The door is open."

"Sir, your dog is sitting on the door step."

Contributed by Sunil Sani, Arooka

No Nepotism

*T*he managing director of a large company sent for his personnel manager and told him, "My son will be graduating from an engineering college next month. I want you to take him on as your assistant. But mind you, I don't want you to show any favouritism towards him. Treat him as you would treat any other of my sons."

Contributed by R. N. Lakhotia, New Delhi

The Reason Why

An MLA went to his party president and said that he wanted to resign his seat. The president wanted to know the reason. The MLA replied, "There are two reasons. One, our party has been in power for nearly five years and has acquired a very unsavoury reputation. Everybody says that it is going to be defeated in the next elections."

The president remarked, "Don't believe these rumours. Our party has arranged a great deal of money and muscle power for the next elections. I am sure we will not lose."

The MLA got up, saying, "This is the second reason for my resignation."

Contributed by Romilla Chawla, Chandigarh

Fiery Short Cut

"Why is the divorce rate so high in the West and so low in India?" asked a visitor to the country.

"*Kaun jaye kachehrie vacherrie, waqt aur paise barbaad karey* (who wants to waste time and money going to courts)," came the reply. "Husbands in India take a short cut, they burn their wives."

Contributed by Sumeet Chowdhry, New Delhi

A Maulana, a Sardarji and a Maharashtrian Brahmin happened to be in a boat which sprang a leak. The boat began to fill with water and it looked all the three would be drowned. The Maulana prayed to Allah for help: "Great and mighty Allah! Thou art compassionate and merciful. Save thy faithful servant from doom. I promise to say many extra *namaazes* and observe many extra *rozas* (fasts) if my life is saved." Lo and behold! A hand stretched down from the heavens and lifted the Maulana from the sinking boat and dropped him safely on land.

The Sardarji raised his hands to the heavens and cried "Merciful *Wahguru*! Save thy faithful *gursikh* and I promise to have a hundred *akhand paaths*." Lo and behold! another hand stretched down from the heavens and lifted the Sardarji from the sinking boat and dropped him unharmed on the land.

It was the turn of the Maharashtrian Brahmin. He too raised his hands to the heavens and prayed to his favourite deity "O thou Omnipotent and all-wise *Ganpati Bapa*! Save me as those two have been saved by their gods." Lo and behold! *Ganpati* himself came down from the heavens and began to dance the *tandavam* in the boat and make it rock violently. "*Ganpati Bapa*," pleaded the poor Maharashtrian, "if you go on doing this, I'll be drowned."

Replied the God of auspicious beginnings, "You humans drown me every year in rivers and oceans. I will do the same to you."

Contributed by Chetan Seth, Noida

Invisible Loss

A village tailor suddenly decamped leaving his clients in a quandary. "He took my pant piece with him," complained Ram Pall.

"He took my suit length with him," complained Ilahi Baksh.

Banta Singh had a more serious complaint, "*Mera to naap lay kar bhaag gayaa* – he decamped with my measurements."

Contributed by J. P. Singh Kaka, Delhi

Dubious Definitions

A Pakistani prostitute in France: *La whore.*

An N.R.I. (Non-Resident Indian): A Hindustan Lever.

Profit: Proprietors Return On Financial Investment after Taxation.

Indian Filmstars: If they display their assets, producers will recover their liabilities.

Contributed by Pathi Vijay Kumar, Bellary

Pregnant Silence

*I*n the corridor of a government office was a signboard reading "Don't make a noise."

Someone added the following words: "Otherwise we may wake up."

Contributed by Shashank Shekhar, Meerut

*I*n the local club a long argument had been going on about whether or not women should be allowed to do men's jobs.

"Mine is a profession that women can't take up," said the auctioneer.

"A woman would make quite as good an auctioneer as a man," said a strongminded woman.

"How can you imagine an unmarried woman standing up before a crowd and saying, 'Now, gentlemen all I want is an offer!'"

Contributed by Amit Banerjee

Last Item

*A*t a family get-together, a proud father was extolling the qualities of his only son, "My son is a fine sportsman and a splendid all-rounder. He plays centre-forward in football and half-back in hockey..." His friend interrupted and asked, "How about his studies?" The son who was around butted in, and said, "In studies I play right-back."

Contributed by K.R. Prithvi Raj, Bombay

A group of brave souls were having their first lesson in sky-diving, "What if the parachute doesn't open?" asked one meekly.

"That's" said the instructor grimly, "what we call jumping to a conclusion."

Contributed by Shashank Shekhar, Meerut Cantt

*I*t was the morning after, and he sat groaning and holding his head.

"Well, if you hadn't drunk so much last night you wouldn't feel so bad now," the wife said tartly.

——"My drinking had nothing to do with it," he answered. "I went to bed feeling wonderful and woke up feeling awful. It was the sleep that did it!"

Ode to Tau

U.S. Rana of New Delhi has sent me a tribute in Haryanavi doggerel addressed to Chaudhri Devi Lal:

Tanney sher ko bakree banaayaa
Rajiv ka raaj hataayaa
Butey ko jarh say ukhaara

You made a goat out of a tiger
You removed Rajiv from his throne
And uprooted Boota Singh from his roots.

Having praised him, he follows it up with another three lines telling Chaudhry Sahib where he went wrong:

Pher aakhir kar, Tau ray Tau
Tanney thaalee mein chheyd kar kay
Apnee goose bhee cook karaaya

Then at last, O revered big Uncle, *Tau,*
You made holes in your platter
And cooked your own goose.

82

The Swimming Sardar

*S*ardar Banta Singh was Punjab's long distance swimming champion. He had crossed and re-crossed all Punjab's rivers in flood without any difficulty. Somebody told him that if he swam the English Channel, he would earn international fame. So Banta arrived in England and began his swim to France. Half way across the 22-mile channel, he decided he couldn't make it to the French Coast. So he swam the same distance back to England.

Contributed by Vimal Kapoor, Dehra Dun

A general, a colonel and a major were having a heated argument on the subject of sex. The general maintained that sex was 60 per cent work and 40 per cent fun. The colonel said it was 75 per cent work and 25 per cent fun. The major thought it was 90 per cent work and 10 per cent fun. At the height of the argument, a private appeared at the door.

"Let's leave it to him," said the major.

The private listened carefully and said with an air of absolute finality, "If you will pardon me, Sirs, sex is 100 per cent fun and no work at all."

"How do you figure that?" cried the astonished officers.

"It is very simple," said the private. "If there was any work in it at all, you guys would have me doing it for you."

I am sure I have read this poem in some anthology of nonsense verse. I reproduce it for the simple reason that it is easily understood, has amusing rhyme and gives us some idea of the longevity of some animals and birds. It is entitled "In Defence of Drinking"

> The horse and mule live thirty years,
> And nothing know of wines and beers.
>
> The goat and sheep at twenty die,
> With never a taste of Scotch or rye.
>
> The cow drinks water by the ton,
> And at eighteen is mostly done.
>
> The dog at sixteen crashes in,
> Without the aid of rum or gin.
>
> The cat in milk and water soaks,
> Then in twelve short years it croaks.
>
> The modest sober bone dry hen,
> Lays eggs for wogs and dies at ten.
>
> All animals are strictly dry,
> They sinless live and swiftly die.
>
> But sinful ginful rum-soaked men,
> Survive for three score years and ten.
>
> And some of us, the mighty few,
> Stay pickled till we're 92!

Contributed by Vidya Ravindran, Pune

Inflation

*T*he teacher was trying hard to explain the meaning of inflation – galloping rate of price rise without relevance to income levels did not register on the students. So the teacher tried to explain it by giving an example:

"The price of the ticket for entry into Pragati Maidan for the India International Trade Fair is Rs.4 per adult as against 50-paise it was five or six years ago. This is inflation. Did you get it?"

"Yes, Sir, this is trade fair inflation. What about the vast increase in the number of visitors to the trade fair?"

The teacher bewildered for a while replied, "Call it populous inflation."

Contributed by M. Dattatreyulu, Delhi

Laloo's Reply

*G*eorge Bush, Mikhael Gorbachev and Laloo Yadav were discussing socialism. The US president said that it was most prevalent in his country as millionaries and poorer people owned cars. Gorbachev said that it was more visible in USSR as both he and his orderly stood in queues for bread. Laloo Yadav gave a disgusted look and asked why the two were still discussing socialism when his state had already advanced to communism. The two statesmen looked aghast as Yadav explained: "In Bihar, the state has withered away!"

Phoren Qualified

*A*n Indian politician returned home after his first visit to England. Pressmen surrounded him and asked him what it was that he had been impressed with most about the English people.

"They are a very gifted race," replied the politician. "Even a two-year-old child can speak English."

Contributed by Vinay Kapoor, New Delhi

Emergency Call

*"H*urry!" the doctor commanded his teenage daughter, "Put my stethoscope and medicine box in my car. That was an emergency call from someone who says he will die if I do not turn up immediately."

"Papa, that call was not for you but for me," replied the girl saucily.

Contributed by Dr. Rajiv Shaveta, Basti Sheikh

Fifty-Fifty Plus

*S*aid a lady to her friend, "When we got our divorce we divided everything we had equally between us. Two children stayed with me, two went to my ex-husband."

"What happened to the property?" asked a friend.

"That was shared equally between his lawyer and mine." ·

Contributed by J. P. Singh Kaka, New Delhi

Once a Sardarji from the countryside brought his pregnant wife to a doctor for sex determination test. After the check-up doctor told Sardarji "*Kuch nahin hei. Keval hava hei*" (It is nothing but gas). The Sardarji got terribly annoyed and said, "*Kya saala tum sochte ho ki mein keval cycle pump hun.*" (What do you think, I am only a cycle pump?)

Contributed by V.C. Jacob, Ranchi

Corruption has become an integral part of our life. A gentleman, after giving matrimonial advertisement for the proposed marriage of his daughter, went on to visit four applicants for better match-making. The first one he visited was a young lad working as a clerk in the Customs department. His parents told the visiting guest that their boy drew a salary of Rs. 1600 per month and an additional income of Rs. 2000 from 'above'. The other boy visited was a clerk working in Excise and Taxation department. The boy got Rs. 1650 as salary and Rs. 2500 per month from 'above'.

A similar explanation came from a boy's parents who was working as a clerk in B & R department: "Rs. 1600 as salary and Rs. 2000 from 'above'." Last came the turn of an Army sepoy. "The boy is in the Army and gets Rs.1500 as salary per month plus ration and leave travel free," was the reply of his parents. "What about the income from "above"?" the visiting guest asked. *"Uppar sey to bomb hi aatey hain"* (from above only bombs are showered), the Army boy, who was present on the occasion, replied.

Contributed by Kishore Pathanua, Chandigarh

Steal Or Not To Steal

A mother was reprimanding her son for having stolen a pencil from school. The father of the family intervened, "*Beta*, you must not steal at school; if you need anything in the way of stationery, I can always get it for you from the office."

Contributed by J. P. Singh Kaka, New Delhi

Mighty Mouse

*A*nand turned up one morning at the office with a big plaster cast stuck across his face.

"What happened?" asked his friend.

"I had an argument with my wife and she beat me up!" replied Anand.

"Beat you up?" his friend exclaimed in shocked tones. "What are you *yaar*, a man or a mouse?"

"I am a man!" asserted Anand.

"And how do you say that?" asked his friend.

"Because," Anand replied, "my wife is afraid of mice."

Contributed by Rajeshwari Singh, New Delhi

Sir C. R. Reddy

*T*he following anecdote illustrates the ready wit of Cuttamanchi Ramalinga Reddy, Founder Vice-Chancellor of the Andhra University. Professor K. Seshadri writes to say that Reddy remained a bachelor. When asked why, he replied, "There is no need to own a cow when there is plenty of milk available."

The Missing Eye

*S*een on the doors of two toilets of a multi-storey office complex in Connaught Circus: "To let Gents" & "To let Ladies". Needless to say lots of people use them to relieve themselves.

Contributed by S.K. Gupta, New Delhi

*B*rown sahibs have lots of fun spotting out grammar and spelling bloomers on hoardings, ads and brochures put out by their countrymen whose command over English is not as good as theirs. An American friend, Leonard J. Baldgya of the US embassy, has sent a short compilation of items picked up by American students in different parts of Europe. They take as good reading as our Hindish.

In a Bucharest hotel lobby: The lift is being fixed for the next day. During that time we regret that you will be unbearable.

In a Belgrade hotel elevator: To move the cabin, push button for wishing floor. If the cabin should enter more persons, each one should press a number of wishing floor. Driving is then going alphabetically by national order.

In a hotel in Athens: Visitors are expected to complain at the office between the hours of 9 and 11 am daily.

In a Japanese hotel: You are invited to take advantage of the chamber-maid.

In the lobby of a Moscow hotel across from a Russian orthodox monastery: You are welcome to visit the cemetery where famous Russian composers, artists, and writers are buried daily except Thursday.

In an Austrian hotel catering to skiers: Not to perumbulate the corridors in the hours of repose in the boots of ascension.

On the menu of a Polish hotel: Salad a firm's own make; limpid red beet soup with cheesy dumplings in the form of a finger; roasted duck let loose; beef rashers beaten up in the countrypeople's fashion.

In a Bangkok dry cleaner's shop: Drop your trousers here for best results.

Outside a Paris dress shop: Dresses for street-walking.

Outside a Hong Kong dress shop: Ladies have fits upstairs.

In an advertisement by a Hong Kong dentist: Teeth extracted by the latest Methodists.

In a Czechoslovakian tourist agency: Take one of our horse-driven city tours – we guarantee no miscarriages.

Detour sign in Kyushi, Japan: Stop – Drive Sideways.

In a Swiss mountain inn: Special today – no ice cream.

In a Bangkok temple: It is forbidden to enter a woman, even a foreigner, if dressed as a man.

In a Tokyo bar: Special cocktail for the ladies with nuts.

In a Copenhagen airline office: We take your bags and send them in all directions.

In a Rome laundry: Ladies, leave your clothes here and spend the afternoon having a good time.

A translated sentence from a Russian chess book: A lot of water has been passed under the bridge since this variation has been played.

In a Rhodes tailor shop: Order your summers suit. Because is big rush we will execute customers in strict rotation.

In an East African newspaper: A new swimming pool is rapidly taking shape since the contractors have thrown in the bulk of their workers.

Advertisement for donkey rides in Thailand: Would you like to ride on your own ass?

In the window of a Swedish furrier: Fur coats made for ladies from their own skin.

Two signs from a Majorcan shop entrance: English well talking. Here speeching American.

From a brochure of a car rental firm in Tokyo: When passenger of foot heave in sight, tootle the horn. Trumpet him melodiously at first, but if he still obstacles your passage then tootle him with vigour.

To the best of my knowledge the only Indian around whom a veritable corpus of linguistic gaffes has grown up is retired Field Marshal K. M. Cariappa, now in the 93rd year of his life and a permanent resident in a hospital in Bangalore.

Cariappa is the archetype of the Brown Sahib, more Sahib than Brown. Though a Coorgi I doubt if he can speak Coorgee or any other Indian language. Cariappaisms started with his alleged speech to the *Jawans* when he took over as Commander-in-Chief of the Indian Army on Independence.

Apparently he was not aware of the difference between being politically free and getting something free of charge. So he commenced his oration with proclamation *"Aaj ham sab log muft ho gaya –* today we can be had for free." For a Sikh gurdwara *"Sikh log ka girjaghar."* There are many others.

A lot of Cariappaisms are in circulation. No one is sure whether they are authentic because no one has checked them with the old soldier. He keeps a stiff upper lip.

Forward To

*B*anta Singh was going on a month's tour and instructed his wife about handling and keeping track of the post that would be delivered while he was away. "Just make a note when the letter is received." When he returned, he found a sizeable pile on his table. Every envelope bore the legend in his wife's hand "Just received".

Contributed by J. P. Singh Kaka, New Delhi

Shrinking Business

A garment shop put a hoarding to advertise the durability of its goods. It read: "*Dada khareedey, pota bartey* – grandpa buys it, grandson wears it."

An old man brought a shirt from the shop. After a few days he came back and complained that after the first wash the shirt had shrunk so much that he could not wear it. "That advertisement is totally false," he said.

"Not at all, Sir," replied the shopkeeper. "You gave it one wash, it became the right size for your son. Your son will wear it for a few days and give it a second wash. Then it will fit your grandson."

Contributed by Veereshwar Sobti, New Delhi

For Cool Customers

*N*otice outside a wayside *dhaba* in Punjab:
"Tehal Singh
Fully air-conditioned."

93

The Reason Why

*Q*uestion: "Why doesn't Mrs. Advani use *Dalda* for cooking her meals?"

Answer: "Because her husband prefers *Rath*."

Contributed by Rajeshwari Singh, New Delhi

All Inclusive Hospitality

A party on a visit to a wildlife sanctuary wishing to spend the night there approached the lodge-keeper. "Are there any rooms available for the night?" they said.

"Rooms available," replied the keeper.

"Any food available?" they asked.

"Yes, food available," he replied.

"Will transport be available tomorrow morning?"

"Transport available."

"What about mosquitoes?"

"Mosquitoes also available," replied the lodge-keeper.

Contributed by Dr. K. P. Misra, Madras

L For Learner

A passenger got into a taxi driven by a Sikh. "Sardarji, please be very careful with your driving; this is the first time I am sitting in a car."

"Not to worry," assured the taxi-driver. "It also happens to be the first time that I am driving a car."

Contributed by J. P. Singh Kaka, New Delhi

Indian Paradise

A school teacher pointed to the painting of Adam and Eve hung on the wall and asked, "Can you tell me which country they are from?"

A student replied, "Sir, they are without clothes, without shelter and have only one apple to eat, still they call it paradise. They must be Indians."

Contributed by Rajnish, Sirmaur

Catchy Signs

Sign outside a tutorial school in Meerut Cantonment: "Expert Kotching in English given here."

Notice in a DTC bus: "Eve-teasing is an offence. Passengers are requested to cooperate."

Outside a Department Store in Connaught Place: "Please note that we shall not be responsible for any rotten stuff unless it bears our label."

A store advertising a new brand of cold-cough syrup: "Got a cold? Try our cough drops. We guarantee you'll never get better."

Sign outside a Theka (liquor vend) in Meerut in Hindi: "If you drink to forget everything, kindly pay us in advance."

On the rear window of a car (enroute to Dehradun from Meerut): Always drive in such a way that your licence expires before you do."

Contributed by Shashank Shekhar, Meerut Cantt

Wedding Anniversary

*I*t was Santa Singh's wedding anniversary. "Shall we have *tandoori* chicken to celebrate the occasion?" Mrs. Santa Singh asked her husband.

"Why take it out on a poor chicken for a mistake we made," replied Santa Singh.

Contributed by J. P. Singh Kaka, New Delhi

*W*hen dying, Mr. Smith told his wife, "Be faithful to my memory or I shall turn in my grave." A year later Mrs. Smith, reached her heavenly abode and enquired about her husband, Mr. Smith. Gabriel told her, "Madam, there are a million named Smith. Is there anything you can further relate to identify him." "Oh yes, my husband said he would turn in his grave if I was not faithful to his memory," Mrs. Smith replied. "Oh! you mean spinning wheel Smith."

Contributed by A. P. Gibbs, Hyderabad

Australian Duck

*N*avjot Siddhu was flown out to Australia for the Christmas Day test. He went for a duck. Why? Because he mistook the duck for the Australian turkey.

Contributed by K. Chandramurti, New Delhi

Telephone Disease

T. Govindan of New Delhi writes about his experience trying to make an STD call to Bombay. He went to his friend Javed who is personal assistant to a Joint Secretary of the Government. "Do you have an STD?" he asked Javed. "No, not at all," replied Javed emphatically. "But you are with a Joint Secretary; you should have an STD," said Govindan.

"Why the hell should I have an STD?" demanded Javed angrily.

"Nothing to get so upset about," said Govindan, "all Joint Secretaries have STD telephones."

"Why didn't you say you wanted to use Subscriber Trunk Dial?" replied Javed, "I thought you wanted to know if I had Sexually Transmitted Disease."

Fat Problem

*D*r. K. P. Misra cardiologist of Madras, was lecturing on the dangers of obesity; being overweight can lead to high blood pressure and heart trouble. "Obesity is like your savings account," said the learned doctor to make things easier for his audience. "There are only two ways of reducing your savings account; either make your deposits smaller or spend more out of it. The same way you can reduce obesity by eating less or spending more by taking exercise which reduces accumulated fat."

A fat banker raised his hand to ask a question.

"Doctor, my problem is I don't have a savings account, I only have a fixed deposit."

98

A young lady went to a hospital and told the receptionist that she wished to see an upturn. "You mean an intern, don't you dear?" asked the kindly nurse. "Well, whatever you call it, I want a contamination," replied the girl. "You mean examination," corrected the nurse. "Maybe so," allowed the girl. "I want to go to the Fraternity ward." "Maternity ward," said the nurse with a slight smile. "Look," insisted the girl, "I don't know much about big words, but I do know that I haven't demonstrated for two months, and I think I'm stagnant."

Inland England

*T*ehl Singh did not know any English. And often mixed up the few words he knew. One day he went to the post office and asked: *"Babuji ik England deyna."* The clerk gave him a foreign air letter form and asked for Rs.5. *"Babuji,* I have always been paying 50-paise for it; why are you charging me Rs. 5 today?"

"Tehl Singhji, you don't mean England, you mean nland," explained the clerk.

"Ikko gal hai" (it is much the same thing), replied Tehl Singh without a blush.

Contributed by Shivtar Singh Dalla, Ludhiana

News-Flash

*T*hieves escaped with over half a million dollars from a bank last night. Police are baffled trying to figure out the motive for the crime.

Contributed by Rajan Sharma, Mukerian

*S*anta Singh and Banta Singh were employed as chauffeurs by two different Cabinet Ministers. They were comparing notes about their duties. *"Yaar Banta, teyree tay mauj hee mauj hay."* (You have lots of fun). *"Tere Minister phoren rahinda"* (Your minister is always abroad).

"No, no," protested Banta, *"maheenay vich do vaar phoren janda* (he goes abroad only twice a month) 1st to 15th and then 15th to the 30th."

Contributed by J. P. Singh Kaka, New Delhi

Sporting Minister

A minister after giving away prizes at a football match made a hard-hitting speech: "Ladies and gentlemen, for the last one hour I have been watching the match. I am sorry to say that even after 43 years of Independence, the federation could provide only one ball to twenty players and the poor players were left with no option but to kick it from one side to the other. I would request the government to give a good grant to the federation so that they could provide one ball to each player so that they can play it the way they like."

Contributed by Promode Kapoor, New Delhi

*J*udge asked the two accused "Couldn't you settle your case, out of court."

"We were trying to, but the police came and arrested us," they said.

Ranga

Once Winston Churchill was delivering a lecture. During his speech, a beautiful lady stood up and asked Churchill a question. Having no appropriate answer to give, he sat down. Another gentleman reminded Churchill that he hadn't answered her question. Promptly came the reply from Churchill, "When skirts go up pants go down."

Contributed by M. L. Aneja, Karnal

A Hindi teacher asked his students *"Kaal kitni prakaar kay hotey hain?"*

Ganga Singh replied, *"Kaal* five type *kay hote hain. Bhoot kaal, Veratmaan kaal, Bhavishyat kaal*, Trunk Call *aur Sat Sri Akal."*

Contributed by J. P. Singh Kaka, New Delhi

Long Vision

*A*n opthalmologist asked a patient, "Tell me, how far can you see?"

Came the reply: "When I get up in the morning, I can see the Sun quite clearly. And, it is said that the Sun is more than nine crore miles away."

Contributed by Prof S. N. Dhar, New Delhi

Fire Hazard

*S*moking is common in Haryana Roadways buses. Once a Sardarji found himself in one. When the man sitting next to him lit his *bidi*, another passenger admonished him: *"Bhai Choudhri! bidi na piye, dhorey Sirdarji baithey."* (Brother Choudhry don't smoke sitting next to a Sardarji.)

Prompt came the reply: *"Sirdarji koi petrol kee tankee sai, jo aag lag jaagee."* (Is Sardarji a petrol tank that might catch fire!)

Contributed by S. Choudhary, Pehowa

Dhumrapaan Nishedh

*T*he Chaudhary of a village was smoking his *hookah* through a two-metre long pipe. When a friend asked him why he had so long a pipe, the Chaudhary replied, "I am following the doctor's advice. He told me to keep my distance from tobacco."

Contributed by J. P. Singh Kaka, New Delhi

Prompt Service

*S*hingari Lal went to a restaurant to have a meal. After a lot of shouting he was able to draw the attention of a waiter who in return spoke loudly and rudely to him. Shingari Lal complained angrily to the manager, "This chap took no notice of me for a long time and then spoke rudely to me."

The hotel manager reprimanded the waiter, "*Bewakoof!* this gentlemen has been barking like a dog for an hour and you took no notice of him. If you carry on like this, not a dog will come to eat here."

Contributed by Shivtar Singh Dalla, Ludhiana

Out Of Focus

A photographer was called to take a picture of a deceased person. After focussing he asked the son of the deceased person to remove the cloth from the face and said, "Smile please!"

Contributed by Sham Keswani, New Delhi

103

For Dogs Only

A young girl acquired a puppy. She went to the bazaar to buy a metal saucer to keep drinking water for her pet. "If it is for your dog," said the obliging shopkeeper, "I can have its name put on it free of charge; so that no one else uses it."

"Not to bother," replied the little Miss. "My puppy can't read English and Papa doesn't drink water."

Contributed by Prem Anand, Ferozepur

Air Conditioned Hell

A rich man on his death bed asked his wife to bury him without any clothes on. "I know which way I'm going," he explained. "I won't need clothes up there!"

When he passed away, his wife kept her promise. A few days later, just as the widow was preparing to go to bed one evening, the man's ghost appeared through the window and said, "Get out my winter underwear and my tweed overcoat, darling. There are so many rich people in Hell now, they've installed air-conditioning."

Contributed by Mehtab Ali Amrohvi

*S*een etched on a desk in a lecture room of a college, "In loving memory of all those who died waiting for this period to be over."

Contributed by Anupama Joseph, Delhi

In The Name Of Ali

A naatak company planning to enact the story of Ramayana was looking out for a really big man who could play the role of Hanuman. Ultimately they found a Pathan well over six feet tall and powerfully built. He was told that he would have to lift a model of a mountain on which grew the *Sanjeevnee bootee*. He agreed to do so for a fee. Came the day for his performance. His face was painted red and a long tail was fixed to his buttocks. He came roaring on the stage and tried to pick up the model mountain. It was too heavy. He tried once, twice and then a third time he put in all the strength he had and picked it as he yelled, "Ya Ali!"

Contributed by Tahira Niazi, New Delhi

Tamil Hindi

A Tamilian eager to learn the national language, asked his friend Heeramath to teach him how to read and write Hindi. He turned out to be a very good student and within a fortnight was able to read Devnagari. They happened to be travelling to Delhi: Heeramath in the upper bunk, the Tamilian on the lower. To test his friend's proficiency Heeramath kept asking him to read out the names of stations they were passing through. The Tamilian kept announcing loudly "Kanpur, Aligarh, Agra." It became dark and the train pulled up at another station. "Where are we?" asked Heeramath from the upper berth. The Tamilian peered out and replied, "*Shauchalaya*".

Contributed by Rajnish, Giri Nagar

Lying Champion

"People say you are the world's greatest liar," said an old hag to a man notorious for never telling the truth.

"I may be," replied the man, "but let me tell you, there is no another woman to match you in looks – *thaara jawaab nahin*."

"How people can malign others!" said the hag. "They can make the most truthful person into a liar – *ek acchey khaasey admee ko badnaam kar key rakh diya*."

Contributed by Shashank Shekhar, Meerut

Siesta Time

One hot afternoon our Professor of Physics was going on and on about the working of hydraulic brakes. Most of the class was getting drowsier and drowsier. A boy in the front row fell asleep. The Professor angrily remonstrated, "All of you look at this fellow. While I am lecturing, he is relaxing." The attention of the class riveted on him, woke the hapless student.

The Professor asked him, "You were not paying any attention. Tell me what was the last word I used?"

"Relaxing, Sir," replied the boy.

Contributed by Supriya Anand, New Delhi

Sir, my wife said I might ask you for a raise."
"Well, I'll ask my wife if I may give you one."

Filmi Gossip

*A*fter Rekha married Mukesh Agarwal, her chief rival in the film world, Sridevi, was eager to outdo her. She received a proposal from a handsome business magnate of the name of Mr. Lal. Sridevi turned down the proposal without bothering to even look at the man. When asked the reason why she had done so, she replied, "I don't wish to be known as Sri Devi Lal."

Contributed by V. Shiv Kumar, Delhi

Permanent Pregnancy

*T*his is a true story of a sweepress working on daily wages in the maternity ward of the Roshan Lal Charitable hospital. She kept hearing the word "pregnant" from doctors and nurses. Her fellow sweepresses were made permanent but she was kept on daily wages. One day she stormed into the office and shouted, "Other sweepresses, Shanti, Kanta and Kamla have been made pregnant. I have been working for six months and no one has made me pregnant."

Contributed by Dr. P. S. Sharma, Delhi

Heard At SJP Headquarters

*T*he Kashmir militants tried to kidnap one of Devi Lal's loved ones but gave up: they couldn't decide which buffalo to take hostage.

Contributed by A Chandra Shekhar Loyalist

107

A footwear shop-owner sold a brown pair of shoes to a young man who was highly delighted with his purchase. Next day he re-entered the shop, returned the pair of shoes and got his money back. "My girl doesn't like it," he explained. A week later, to the shop-owner's surprise, the young man breezed in and bought the same pair of shoes again. "Has your girl changed her mind?" the shop-owner asked him. "No," he smiled. "I've changed the girl."

Contributed by Reeten Ganguly, Tezpur

*S*ome years ago I was travelling in summer by a mail bus in north-west Rajasthan. It had to frequently stop as the tyres got struck in sand deposited on the road by the wind. Irritated, a lady burst out "Who said this bus is mail? It is not even female."

Contributed by Kanti C. Singhee, Chittorgarh

A school inspector asked the class, "If length of the platform is 200 metres and speed of the train is 100 kilometres what should be my age?" Noting the absurdity of the question, a clever student answered, "Fifty years, sir." The answer was absolutely correct. The inspector was astounded. He asked the boy his method of calculation. "Simple, sir," the boy replied, ."I have an elder brother aged 25 years and everybody calls him half mad!"

Contributed by Baldev Kapur, New Delhi

*T*wo rival authors met. One had just published a book. Said the other, "I read your book and thought it was great. Tell me, who wrote it for you?"

The author replied, "I'm so glad you enjoyed it. Tell me, who read it for you?"

Contributed by Rose Sands

Indian Similes

*H*ere are a few examples of some apt similes for Indian situations:

Options in Indian politics: Like putting Band-Aid on a patient afflicted with a third stage cancer.

Newspaper photographer: Like a lottery maniac who draws by a dozen in a fond hope that at least one will click.

Indian politician: Stray dog, who gets noticed only when he makes a complete nuisance of himself or when a powerful leader decides to adopt him by putting a collar around his neck.

Morarji Desai: Like a cab driver in Connaught Place honking full volume with both doors of his car open.

Dangerous: As terrorist Jinda asking a date from Home Minister's daughter for a walk at night by the sea side.

Ancient Indian Culture: Like sagging breasts of an old woman; largely reminiscent and in need of support.

Night: So quiet that you could hear a cricket clear its throat with Vicks cough drops.

Reshuffling the Cabinet: Like kicking some stray dogs so that their food could be given to other dogs.

General elections: Like telling a voter going to the electric chair that he has a choice between AC and DC.

Nationalism: As deep as ringing up 176 (Special Information) on 15th August to find out why it is a public holiday.

Unlikely: As Win Chaddha not knowing what a hundred rupee note looks like.

Contributed by Vishv Bandhu, New Delhi

Buttons Are Safer

A mother took her young son to a tailor to have trousers made for him. After taking the boy's measurements, the tailor asked the mother whether he should put buttons in front or a zip fastener which was more the fashion. The mother paused a while before replying. "He has a zip on his cardigan and he often gets his neck-tie caught in it. I think it would be safer if he has buttons on his pants."

Contributed by P. P. Singh, Chandigarh

The Reason Why

*A*n Indian Airlines advertisement asks "Why does the world's second largest domestic airlines charge the world's lowest fare?"

Arun Agarwal of Patna has given an apt reply "Because it offers the worst service in the world."

More Mobile Wisdom

*A*n autorickshaw bears the following slogan:
Sharaabee dey do thikaaney
Ik theykey, dooja thaaney
A drunkard has two abodes,
The tavern and the police station.

Contributed by J. P. Singh Kaka, New Delhi

Friend in Need

A father was worried about his son's ability to pass his English essay test. So he made him cram one on 'My Best Friend' which he was sure would be one of the choices. Instead of that the subject on the examination paper was 'My Father'. Undaunted, the boy utilised his memorised text to his best advantage. His essay read "I have many fathers. Ravi Prasad is my best father. He lives next door to us. He comes to visit us everyday. My mother loves him very much. A father in need is a father indeed."

Contributed by Saket Budhiraja, New Delhi

*A*n ingenious ad put up by a *kulfiwalla* at a cross road:

Bhai Sahib, aap deykhtey kidhar hain?
Kamal Singh kee kulfian idhar hain.
(Dear brother, why are you looking that way?
Kamal Singh's *kulfis* are on this way.)

Contributed by Bhavana Mathur, New Delhi

"*C*an you tell me what steam is?" asked the examiner.

"Why sure, Sir," replied the student confidently. "Steam is – why – er – it is water that is gone crazy with the heat."

Contributed by Rajan Sharma, Mukerian

Diplomat: A person who thinks twice before saying nothing.

Politician: Someone who shakes your hand before election – and your confidence afterwards.

Husband: A person who is under the impression that he bosses the house when, in reality, he only houses the boss.

Television: A chatter-box that presents programmes that give you a headache and then advertises a cure for it.

Friendship: A relationship that involves lending you an umbrella by someone but taking it back when it begins to rain.

Chaperon: An elderly woman who accompanies young women to ensure that they don't commit any such mistake she committed when she was herself young.

An economist: Someone who thinks more about money than the people who have it.

Childhood: When you make funny faces in the mirror.

Middle age: When the mirror gets even.

Contributed by Shashank Shekhar, Meerut Cantt

*E*pitaph on a rich man's tomb. "I struggled with arithmetic all my life. As a child, I learned to add. As a young man, I was a master at multiplying. As an adult I never learned to subtract. And now my relatives will divide."

*C*orbusier, the architect of Chandigarh, als designed its 11-storeyed Secretariat. He designed tw ramps for entering the building. When asked why he ha two instead of one, he replied: "So that employee leaving early do not collide with those coming in late. After the building was completed it was noted that ther was no possibility of any collisions as employees wh came in late were the ones who left early.

Contributed by P. S. Chawla, Chandigar

Yamadoo

A poor old widow carrying a load of firewood o her head was on her way back home. Ṣhe got very tire and cried loudly, "Yama, you relieve other people of thei burdens by taking them away, why do you forget thi wretched old woman?" Suddenly Yama appeared ridin; his bull, "Come along *Mai*, I heard your plea. Get on th bull behind me."

"No *beta*," pleaded the woman, "I only wante someone to help me put this bundle of firewood on m head. I managed to do it myself."

Contributed by Arun Buxi, Jalandh

*A*n infant does not enjoy infancy as much as a adult enjoys adultery.

Contributed by A. P. Gibbs, Hyderab

KEEP YOUR FAMILY SMALL
USE THE RIGHT TYPE OF LUBRICANT

A signboard at a petrol pump in South Calcutta boldly exhorts people to "Keep your family small". And beneath this national slogan is given another advice, albeit less prominently, "Use the right type of lubricant".

Contributed by Kanti C. Singhee, Chittorgarh

*S*een on the back of a truck the following message:
Yeh trolley nahin, mohabbat ka phool hai
Wazan utna hee dalo, jitna usool hai
This is not a trolley but the flower of love,
Load it as permitted by the law.

Another message reads:
Maalik kaa paisa, driver ka paseena
Niklee hai sarak pay, ban kay hassena
The boss's money, the driver's sweat
She's on the road, decked in her best.

Contributed by Manoj Seth, Sirsa

Question of Copyright

*Q*uestion: "Why did K. S. (Khushwant Singh) sue the company which makes Kama Sutra condoms?"
Answer: "Because the ad. only says 'Ask for K.S.'"

Contributed by Vijay Asawa, Calcutta

Familiar Face

A Haryanavi youth spied a pretty girl at the bus stand. Since no one was around, he tried to use a tone of familiarity, "*Jaan-e-man* – my heart's desire," he addressed her, "*aisee laagey sai, aap ko pehley kahin dekha sai.*"

"*Jaroor deykha sai* – you must have seen me," replied the lady, "I am a nurse at the lunatic asylum."

Contributed by Shashank Shekhar, Meerut

116

Desi Anda

A grey-bearded Sardarji boarded the Air India flight to London carrying a basket in his arms which he held close to his chest. He pressed the call-button to summon the stewardess. "*Bibi*," he addressed the girl kindly, "are you sure our pilot knows how to fly the plane properly? Do find out if he has a driving licence and has taken enough petrol for the journey." The girl assured him that the Captain was an experienced pilot and had taken enough fuel to get the plane to London.

A few minutes later he pressed the call bell again and asked the girl: "Find out if the engine was properly overhauled before we left and there is enough air in the tyres. Did he check them for punctures?" the girl reassured him again and asked: "*Babaji* why are you worried about your life? We will get you safely to London."

"I'm not worried about myself," the old man replied, "I am worried about what I am carrying in this basket. You see I have a son living in Southhall and he has written to me about tasteless battery produced eggs of England. So I am taking a few dozen eggs of *desi murgees* and I don't want them to get smashed on the way."

Contributed by Manmohan Singh, New Delhi

*I*n Aurangabad, 1968, in conjunction with the sisters of the Holy Cross, I was organist and choirmaster for a Christmas Carol Service. A number of officials were invited to read selected portions from the Scriptures. One portion: 'The treasures will be opened and the glories of God will be revealed' was read as: 'The trousers will be opened and the glories of God will be revealed.'

Contributed by A. P. Gibbs, Hyderabad

117

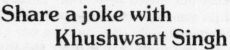

Share a joke with Khushwant Singh

If you have a joke, a humorous anecdote or a funny incident, which is original and you would like to share it with Khushwant Singh and his million admirers, send it to us today. If selected, it would be printed in the next edition of Khushwant Singh's Joke Book.

... and a million others

Remember

- Each joke or anecdote must be neatly typed or written on a separate sheet of paper in about 125-150 words.
- Do not type or write on both sides of the sheet. Write on one side only.
- Send your jokes to :

    Khushwant Singh's Joke Book
    c/o **Orient Paperbacks**
    Madarsa Road, Kashmere Gate
    DELHI - 110 006

- Each contribution received would be acknowledged.
- Each selected contribution would be acknowledged and included in the next edition of **Khushwant Singh's Joke Book** along with the name of the contributor.

Price of Fame

Mr. V. S. Khandekar was a famous Marathi writer who wrote many novels and short stories. Once his youngest son came from school much earlier than usual. On being questioned he told his father that a famous leader died and his school declared holiday as a respect to the departed soul.

It occured to the boy that his father was also very famous so he asked him, "Daddy, you are also a very famous man. Will we get holiday if you die?"

Mr. Khandekar replied, "I am not sure whether everybody will get a holiday, but I am sure you will certainly get a holiday."

Contributed by Prabhakar S. Harsole, Indore

A young priest complained to his senior, that in the course of his sermon, he observed many in the congregation slept. The senior advised him to shock the congregation, "Mention that you slept in the arms of another man's wife. When they are fully alert mention that it was your mother." So the next Sunday, finding the congregation asleep he mentioned that last night he slept in the arms of another man's wife. When the congregation was fully alert, the priest became nervous and said, he had forgotten the name of the woman.

Contributed by A. P. Gibbs, Hyderabad

Military Imprecision

*S*ome ladies who were determined to put an end to drinking in their colony, went to the house of a retired Army Officer one evening.

"When did you last have a drink?" they asked.

"1945" replied the officer.

"That is very good!" remarked the ladies very happily. "So you are a teetotaller now?"

"I wouldn't call it exactly that," replied the officer looking at his watch. "You see it is only 2015 now."

Contributed by Rajeshwari Singh, New Delhi

Heal Thyself

*T*his incident took place in one of the special clinics of the All India Institute of Medical Sciences, New Delhi. A patient with an asthmatic complaint visited the afternoon clinic starting at 2 p.m. Being a man of influence he was allowed into the Senior Consultant's room for check-up. A junior doctor asked him several questions which the patient answered. Then the Senior Consultant was briefed by his junior. The senior asked the patient to lie down on a couch and examined him thoroughly. He asked, "Are you a smoker?"

"I was..."

"Do you drink...?"

After some hesitation, the patient answered, "Yes" As the patient was leaving the senior doctor warned him against drinking and smoking. Then he got out his packet of cigarettes and asked him, *"Suniye saab aap ke pass matches hoge?"*

Contributed by Mohan Menon, New Delhi

Ranga

A minister was having his morning walk along with his dog. A member of the opposition party happened to walk by. He asked, "How come you are strolling with a donkey?" The minister was very angry, he said "Can't you see, this is a dog, not a donkey." The other replied, "I didn't ask you, I was talking to the dog."

Contributed by Surjit Sethi, Dimapur

Paradise Lost

*H*ere is an anecdote to illustrate the difference between illusion and reality of living abroad. Sardar Santa Singh arrived at the gates of paradise and what he saw pleased him immensely: people riding large limousines, casino, night clubs, preety girls in bikinis and liquor bars. When presented before God he expressed his delight to be there. God looked up his record and said "Santa, there has been a terrible mistake. You are not due here till four years later. You go back to earth and we will send for you on the right time."

Santa Singh went back. He looked forward to returning to paradise. When he finally died and appeared at the pearly gates, the sight that met his eyes was different: men sweeping gardens, cutting wood and doing back-breaking jobs. Women scrubbing floors, cooking, washing dishes and soiled garments.

"This is not the paradise you showed me last time," he protested to God.

"Last time you came on a tourist visa," replied the Almighty. "This time you came on an immigrant visa."

Contributed by Ranju Kohli, Washington D.C.

Death Duties

B. S. Kalra of New Delhi writes that there had been a succession of death of male relatives and he had to give money to their widows as customary. When he was telling his wife how much out of pocket he was, she assauged his feelings by saying "Don't worry, it will all come back to me when I become a widow."

Special Eyes

A shopkeeper's son had trouble with his eyes. He took the boy to an eye-specialist who operated upon and replaced the boy's eyes with those donated by a Minister.

A few days after the operation, the doctor asked the father, "How's your son doing?"

"He is fine," replied the father, "but he keeps on gazing at a chair whenever he finds one."

Contributed by Firoz Bakht Ahmed, Delhi

The Masculine Touch

G ermaine Greer, leader of the feminist movement, called on the law-giver Manu and chastised him for his discriminatory laws against women, "Can you give me one good reason for prescribing that women should walk ten paces behind men?" she demaned.

"Dearest *kanya!*" replied the sage "at first, women used to walk ahead of their men. Then incidents of bottom pinching became so rampant that I had to make new rules. I prescribed ten paces distance between the two to make women's posteriors beyond the reach of men. I did so not to discriminate against women but to protect them."

Ms. Greer, who had been in Italy before she came to see Manu, complimented Manu for his sagacity.

Contributed by Ashesh Ghose, Bombay

Drink or Death

*S*een behind a three-wheeler in Delhi was the following message:

Hey dost, Bhagwan say maut dilaa dey;
Ya Bhagwan sey kah roz pilaadey

Friend, ask God to grant me death I pray
Or tell Him to give me a drink everyday.

Contributed by Vinay Kapoor, New Delhi

Half Drunk

*A*man saw his friend limping badly as he came towards him. "*Yaar*, how did you come by this injury to your leg?"

"I did not have enough to drink," replied the other.

"That does not make any sense! How can you hurt yourself by not having enough to drink?"

"Very simple," replied his friend, "if I had been really and fully drunk, I would have fallen down at the *theyka*. As I was half drunk, I tried to walk home, fell into a ditch and sprained my foot."

Contributed by Gurdeep Singh Chugh, Paonta Sahib

A man lost his ring and reported the matter to the police. While police started their usual enquiries, the man, traced his ring from his pants. He immediately reported to police.

"What the hell are you talking about. We have already caught fourteen criminals and six of them have already confessed the theft," replied the police inspector.

*T*he middle-aged woman went to see her doctor. "Well, what's the trouble?"

"Doctor, it's headache; shooting pains in my legs and high blood pressure."

"How old are you?" asked the doctor.

"I'll be 26 on my next birthday."

"H'mm," said the doctor, busy writing, "loss of memory too."

Contributed by Shashank Shekhar, Meerut Cantt

Piggy Back

*M*r. and Mrs. Banta Singh's two-year-old boy was bawling away loudly. Mrs. Singh asked her husband why their son was being so difficult. "He wants to take a ride on a donkey," replied Banta.

"Then why don't you put him on your shoulders and go for a run?"

Contributed by J. P. Singh Kaka, New Delhi

*W*hen seeking admission to the celestial abode, the care taker angel gave me a piece of chalk directing me to mark a cross upon each step of the ladder for each sin committed. I was consciously complying accordingly, ascending. I accosted a beautiful vivacious lady, elegantly attried, descending and asked, "Why, have you not been accorded admission?" She merely replied, "The chalk is finished.

Contributed by A. P. Gibbs, Hyderabad

When tenders were floated for the channel tunnel to connect England and France, many international building companies vied with one another to get the contract. The stakes were very high; the job of digging beneath the sea required great engineering skill and building expertise. Tenders were opened by the Board of Directors of the Anglo-French Corporation which had taken on the project. British builders' estimates were over 200 million dollars each; French and German builders were marginally lower. There was one from India: Singh & Singh Builders whose estimate was only 5 million dollars. The Board was for ignoring the Indian tender but out of curiosity invited Singh & Singh over to discuss the plans.

Banta Singh and Santa Singh of Singh & Singh Builders appeared before the Board. The Chairman asked them "Have you any experience of undertaking this kind of work?"

"Indeed we have," replied the two Singhs, "we bored a lot of tubewells in the Punjab and Haryana. We can bore holes anywhere."

"This is not as simple. How will you connect the tunnel from the English side to the French?"

"Simple," replied Santa Singh, "Banta Singh will dig from the French end and I from the English."

The Chairman was flabbergasted. "You don't realise that it will need a lot of accurate calculation to get the two tunnels to meet at the same point under the channel. Other companies' estimates are over 200 million dollars each and you think you can do the same job for 5 million dollars. How will that be possible?"

"What is bothering you?" demanded Singh & Singh, "if our two tunnels don't meet, instead of one we will give you two tunnels."

Contributed by Prem Khanna, Noida

*T*wo friends Santa Singh and Banta Singh, were always boasting of their parents' achievements to each other.

Santa Singh: "Have you heard of the Suez Canal?"

Banta Singh: "Yes, I have."

Santa Singh: "Well, my father dug it."

Banta Singh: "That's nothing. Have you heard of the Dead Sea?"

Santa Singh: "Yes, I have."

Banta Singh: "Well, my father killed it."

Tit For Tat

A professor was warning his students against the hazards of kissing. "You should know when a boy kisses a girl he transfers 40,000 germs from his mouth to that of his girl friend. What can you do about that?"

Pat came the reply from a girl, "You should give him back all his germs the same way."

Contributed by J. P. Singh Kaka, New Delhi

Ranga.

Cuts Both Ways

A government official was arrested for accepting a bribe from a contractor. A friend who went to visit him in the lock-up asked, "How are you going to get out of this mess?"

The official replied calmly, "I got into trouble for accepting a bribe; I'll get out of it by giving it."

A Sardarji went to a logic school to learn logic. "To begin with, I'll explain you the term logic with the help of an example," the Professor said.

"Do you have a fish pond?" asked the Professor.

"Yes," said Sardarji.

"This means you love fish," the Professor continued.

"Yes."

"That is you love water."

"Yes."

"Everybody drinks water, meaning you love everybody."

"Yes."

"This means you love a boy."

"Yes."

"So you love a girl."

"Yes."

"If you love a girl, then you are a boy."

"Yes, I am a boy."

"And if you are a boy, you are not homosexual."

"Yes, true, I am not a homosexual," said Sardarji.

"So this is the logical relationship between a fish pond and homosexual," the Professor ended.

That night Sardarji could not sleep well and wondered regarding the logical relationship between fish pond and a homosexual. Next day, on his way to the logic school, he met his friend who inquired about his first day at logic school. Sardarji said proudly, "I'll explain you the term logic with the help of an example."

"Do you have a fish pond?" asked Sardarji.

"No," his friend replied.

"Then you are a homosexual," Sardarji concluded.

Contributed by Ashish Bakshi, New Delhi

A reception was held in New Delhi. One of the guests, Home Minister Buta Singh loses his invitation card. He arrrives and explains who he is to the guard at the door.

"But how do I know who you are?" asks the guard. "An hour ago, Ravi Shanker came without his invitation card, I gave him a *sitar* and he played a beautiful *raag*. And half an hour ago, Mani Shanker came without his invitation card, I asked him to name all the recipients of Bofors kickbacks, and he named them all."

"Who is this Ravi Shanker and Mani Shanker?"

"Say no more," says the guard, "you are Buta Singh."

Contributed by Judson K. Cornelius, Hyderabad

Proof Positive

*M*r. and Mrs. Banta Singh went to the Election Commissioner's office. Banta asked the Election Commissioner, "Sir, I want to know whether our name is in the voter's list." The officer checked the list and said, "Sardarji, the list shows you as dead." Banta Singh said, "Sir, I'm standing before you, how can I be dead?" At this Mrs. Banta Singh shouted at her husband, "Shut up. He is an Election Officer, he can't tell a lie."

Contributed by J. P. Singh Kaka, New Delhi

Casual Leave

A newly-employed villager was very weak in English. Once he asked his more educated neighbour to draft an application asking for casual leave for a day as he was down with fever.

The neighbour dictated the application in the following words: "Respected Sir – As I am suffering from fever, I may kindly be granted casual leave for today."

He kept a copy of this application for subsequent use. Later, on the eve of his sister's marriage, he wrote an application on his own. It read as follows: "Respected Sir – As I am suffering from my sister's marriage tomorrow, kindly grant me casual leave for the next two days."

Contributed by Shashank Shekhar, Meerut Cantt.

Election Gimmickry

R R. Sagar of Muzaffarpur narrates a story about an election campaign. A car broke down on the road. While the driver was tinkering with the engine, a rustic came along and asked if he could get a ride to his village which was a short distance away in the same direction. "No," replied the car owner, "this car is only meant to take Congress voters from their villages to the polling booth. You go to your village on foot and then I may give you a lift."

The car drove away. The driver remarked to his boss, "Sir, I am sure from this man's village we will not get a single vote."

"That was the whole idea," replied the boss. "I don't want my party to win because it did not give me the ticket."

A humorist, very confident of his art, claimed that there was no one living who would not laugh at his set of jokes. And if there was a person who did not laugh, he was ready to pay Rs. 1 lakh to such an individual.

Many tried, and went back laughing, but without the prize money. Bhenga Singh went to try his luck. And lo and behold, he did not laugh at all, inspite of the choicest jokes narrated by the humorist. Bhenga Singh got the prize money of Rs. 1 lakh and went home.

After one week, Mrs. Bhenga Singh came back to return the money to the humourist, saying that Bhenga Singh had gone crazy. For the last one week he had been doing nothing but staring at the prize money and laughing.

The humourist was puzzled. He contacted Bhenga Singh to find the reason for his unusual behaviour. "The joke became clear to me only after I reached home," replied Bhenga Singh.

Contributed by S. P. Trehan, Chandigarh

Cricket Debacle

*A*fter its debacle in the recent World Cup cricket the Indian team returned home. Scared of the public ire against its performance, the players decided to stay indoors for some days. Ultimately Srikkant decided to venture out, disguised himself wearing a veil. A lady came and greeted him. Srikkant ran back into hiding. The next day he went out disguised in another costume. Once again the same lady accosted him. Frustrated he asked "How the hell, did you recognise me?" The 'lady' replied "Come on, Sri, that is very easy. I am Ravi Shastri!"

Contributed by Ashok K. Sharma, New Delhi

*T*he preacher in a small town had become very perturbed, and he decided to lay it on the line to the congregation.

"Brothers and sisters," he said solemnly, "it has come to my attention that there are tales to the effect that immorality is rampant in our fair town. To be specific, it is being said that there is not one virgin left here. This vile lie must and shall be refuted. In order to do so, I ask every virgin in the congregation to rise."

Not a women stirred. After a lot of coaxing, a young lady, far in the rear, with a baby in her arms, rose bashfully.

The preacher stared with astonishment at the baby, then said, "Young woman, I am asking virgins to stand."

The young lady answered indignantly, "Well, do you expect this six-month-old girl to stand by herself?"

Contributed by Judson K. Cornelius, Hyderabad

What's in a Caste?

S. S. Jha, Collector of Customs, was once asked by his neighbour K. Chandramurti whether he was a Muslim, a Christain, a Kshatriya or a Sudra. Jha was incensed, "I am amazed at your ignorance! Jhas are Hindu Maithili Brahmins of the highest castes."

"I see, so you are a Hinduja," remarked Chandramurti.

Contributed by K. Chandramurti, New Delhi

133

A young doctor was attached to a senior to gain practical insight into practice. The fresher told the senior that the seniors were not abreast with the latest trend in medical science. The senior advised the young doctor to be observant on the visits. In the first visit, the patient was a young man. After the preliminary examination, the doctor advised the young man to give up smoking. When they were outside the young doctor questioned on what basis he tendered that advise, the senior replied there were cigarette butts, ashes strewn all over the room.

The second patient was a young lady. The senior after completing preliminaries directed her to stop eating sweets and chocolates. Again when questioned, the senior commented he saw chocolate and sweet wrappers strewn in the room. Upon the third visit, the senior surprised the younger doctor requesting him to examine the patient, a young lady. Through sheer nervousness the young doctor dropped the stethoscope. After the preliminaries he advised the young lady to give up all church activities. Later the senior commented upon the younger doctors astuteness and enquired how he had come to that advise. "Oh! when I dropped my stethoscope and picked it up, I saw the priest under the cot," replied the young doctor.

Contributed by A. P. Gibbs, Hyderabad

*W*ife to husband: "How old do you think I look?"
"Twenty, looking at your hair, 19, for your skin, 18 for your joviality, and 17 for your figure."
"Do you really mean that, dear?"
"I sure do. Now, let me add, 20 plus 19, plus..."

Guess What?

*T*here was this village lost in the depth of the Kumaon hills. No one visited it and none of its inhabitants had gone out to see what the rest of the world looked like. Then suddenly one villager won a lottery which gave him a free ticket to see three big cities of India. The entire village was agog with excitement. They gave their co-villager a pen and a pad and said, "You make a note of whatever you see in everyone of the three cities you visit and come and tell us about it when you return."

The lucky villager was first taken to Delhi and shown the Kutub Minar. In his pad he noted down "Kutub Minar". The next city he went to was Jaipur. There he saw many camels and faithfully recorded "camel". The third city was Ahmedabad where he saw lots of donkeys. He recorded "donkey". When he returned to his village, he told everyone of the wonderful things he had seen. Some months later a camel strayed into the village. They ran to the man who had seen the world outside. He came and saw the strange looking beast and pronounced, "It could be the Kutub Minar or it could be a camel or it could as well be a donkey."

Contributed by Mrinal Pande, New Delhi

Baby Food

*Q*uestion: "How could Manmohan Singh accomplish where former Finance Ministers had failed?"

Answer: "When he was a baby he was fed with Forex instead of Farex."

Contributed by Bharat Rajdev, New Delhi

Blissful Ignorance

When the stock exchange index reached its peak before the Harshad Mehta affair broke out, many rich contractors, who knew very little about the stock exchange, used the opportunity to make some quick money. Their level of ignorance can be made out from the following incident, narrated by a broker. One day he received a call from one of these fat cats who wanted to find out about what was happening in the market. The broker says, he told the caller that the index had touched 3, 000 points. Prompt came the reply, *"Theek hai, uske bhi hazaar kharid lo.*(OK, buy a thousand of that too.)"

Silence

Once I was in a public library at Ajmer. A little boy sitting nearby was making much noise. I requested the librarian to tell him to keep quite. The librarian went over to the little boy and said "My dear boy, will you please be quite! Do you know that the people near you can't even read."

The boy asked in wonder, "They can't read; then what are they doing here?"

Contributed by R. N. Lakhotia, New Delhi

Banta Singh: "Er, is that Air-India office? Can you tell me how long it takes to fly from Delhi to Bombay?"
Booking clerk: "Just a minute, Sir..."
Banta: "O.K. Thanks a lot." And he hangs up.

Contributed by Kamal Sharma, Mukerian

Serpentine Attraction

*S*ubhash Lakhotia narrates an amusing experience of his club's meetings at which only tea was served. Few members bothered to come. The Secretary decided to add incentives to ensure better attendance and arranged for snacks to be served with tea. Much to his surprise at the next meeting not a single member turned up. He checked with his clerk whether a proper circular had been sent out in time. The mystery was cleared. The invitation read, "Please note snakes will be served with tea."

Paradisal Justice

*T*hree men who died the same day were presented before God. The almighty showed particular interest in their sex life. The first one replied that he never had an affair before or after he was married. God granted him a chauffeur-driven Cadillac. The second man admitted he had some affairs before he was married but none afterwards. God gave him an Ambassador car. The third man confessed to having had lots of affairs. God gave him a scooter. A few days later the man with the scooter saw the fellow with the chauffeur-driven Cadillac sitting by the roadside and crying. The scooterist asked him why was he upset. Replied the Cadillac owner, "I've just seen my wife ride past on a bicycle."

Contributed by D.K. Saxena, Jaipur

Lame To The One-eyed

Once the lame conqueror, Taimur, was holding a *durbar* on a platform overlooking a public thoroughfare. His eyes fell on a girl carrying a basket full of flowers on her head. He ordered one of his sentries to go and fetch her. The flower-girl was brought before the king. Taimur was surprised to see that this beautiful girl was blind in one eye. He asked her name. "My name is *Daulat*", replied the girl. Taimur remarked, "Can *Daulat* ever be one-eyed?"

The girl retorted, "Had *Daulat* not been one-eyed, how could a lame become a conqueror?"

Contributed by Lassa Kaul, New Delhi

Come Hither

An ingenious ad put up by a *kulfiwalla* at a cross road:

Bhai Sahib, aap deykhtey kidhar hain?
Kamal Singh kee kulfian idhar hain.
(Dear brother, why are you looking that way?
Kamal Singh's *kulfis* are on this way.)

Contributed by Bhavana Mathur, New Delhi

An attorney made this observation after weathering a nasty divorce case: "Marriage is the only union that cannot be organised. Each side thinks it is management."

Nothing To Chatter About

A man got a severe fit of shivering. They put quilts and blankets on him; put a hot water bottle in his bed and lit a fire in his room. But he would not stop shivering. Then someone noticed that while the rest of his body was shivering, his teeth were not chattering. "How is it that while every part of your body is shaking, there is no sound of your teeth chattering?"

The man opened his mouth, bared his gums and explained, "Because my dentures are in a glass of water."

Contributed by Harjeet Kaur, New Delhi

*T*his happened to an American visitor in Madras. In his hotel he picked up the telephone one night and asked for a 7-Up. The switchboard operator answered in his best English, "7-Up? Yes, Sir."

The cold drink never arrived, but the next morning the tourist was woken up punctually at seven o'clock.

Tailpiece

*A*fter the stock scam and subsequent collapse of the stock market a businessman was asked by his friend if he too had done any trading in the market.

"Of course I did," replied the businessman.

"What were you? A bull or a bear?"

"An ass."

*A*man set down three pieces of luggage before the Indian Airlines check-in counter at the Santa Cruz Airport, Bombay. "I want the brown bag to go to Delhi, the black one to Calcutta," he said. "And keep the third bag here till I come back next week and pick it up."

The airline official blinked. A supervisor standing behind the check-in clerk overheard the passenger's request and came up. "I am sorry, but we are not the post office," the supervisor said, "we can't do that."

"Why not?" the irate passenger said, raising his voice, "That's what you did the last time!"

Thanks to Harshad

*D*uring the boom in the share market, my friend Mahesh Lalwani sold all his shares which fetched him Rs. 150,000. With the money he bought a new Maruti and asked me to suggest a suitable slogan to paint on the back of his new car. He accepted my suggestion to paint, "Courtesy Harshad Mehta".

Countributed by R.D. Gera, Delhi

Himachali Paradise

*O*nce the Chief Minister of Himachal Pradesh was addressing a public meeting. He said, "*Bhaiyo, hum Himachal ko Bharat ka Switzerland bana dengay* — we will make Himachal into the Switzerland of India."

A man shouted back, "Then we don't have to put our black money in a Swiss bank — *Yaheen khaata khol lengay* — we can open our account here."

Contributed by Rajnish, Sundernagar

Patriotic Emigration

*T*wo notorious pick-pockets migrated to England and applied for membership of a prestigious Indian society. In the column asking for their qualifications they made the following entry, "True patriots are we, for we left our country for the good of our country."

Contributed by Deepak Bhakoo, Ludhiana

The State of Affairs

A potted version of the state of affairs in our country inscribed behind an autorickshaw:

Jheel par paani barasta hai, hamaarey deysh mein
Kheyt paani ko tarasta hai, hamaarey deysh mein
Zindgee ka haal khasta hai, hamaarey deysh mein
Insaan ka khoon sasta hai, hamaarey deysh mein
Ab leedron, afsaron aur paagalon ko chhor kar
Kaun khul kar hastua hai, hamaarey deysh mein?

The rain fall on lakes in our land
While fields go thirsty in our land
What lives of misery do we live in our land
Human blood is cheap in our land
Now besides leaders, officials and lunatics
No one laughs heartily in our land.

Contributed by Sarbari Mukherjee, New Delhi

A plea for peace:
"No God. No Peace
Know God. Know Peace."

*I*n the Garden of Eden, Adam asked God, "Why did you make Eve so beautiful?"

"To attract your attention."

"Why did you give her such a winsome personality?"

"So that you would love her."

Adam thought about this for a while. "Why, then, did you make her so dumb?"

"So that she would love you!"

Selective Dog Bite

A policeman bitten by a dog came for treatment to the Safdarjang Hospital. He asked the pharmacist, "*Arey bhai! Kuttey katne kee davaa dena* – brother give me medicine for dog bite."

The pharmacist asked him, "*Santree jee! Aap ko bhee kuttey nay kaat liya* – how did a dog bite a policeman?"

The constable replied, "To tell you the truth, I was not wearing my uniform at the time."

Contributed by Veereshwar Sobti, New Delhi

*S*een in the *Indian Express*: "The Periyar National Park has great potential for attaching domestic and foreign tourists."

*T*he breakup of the former USSR and the rapidly changing political scene in East Europe has resulted in a new crop of jokes. Here is one on the 'new' political education (and realities) in former Germany.

"What is the difference between capitalism and socialism?"

"A big difference, comrade."

"And what is it?"

"Under capitalism, man exploits man. Under socialism, it was the other way round."

*"Y*ou should not throw rocks at the police," an American tourist told a Polish demonstrator. "In our country, if we want to protest against someone, we throw tomatoes or eggs."

"If we had tomatoes and eggs," said the Pole, "we wouldn't be protesting."

*T*he income-tax inspectors are notorious around the world. This one was reported in the Financial Times, London.

This tax inspector went back to his office one night and found a burglar rifling his safe. After a fierce struggle the intruder managed to break away and run off. The taxman telephoned the police, and half an hour later they rang back to tell him that they had caught the man and found $30 in his pockets. "I know," he said. "He had $45 on him when he broke in."

143

"Unputdownable"
... The Pioneer

"Funny and Ribald"
... Hindu

"A pain in the belly..."
...Onlooker

Illustrated by Mario Miranda

Rs 50